Faith Without Belief

Faith Without Belief

A Guide for Doubters

Derek S. King

CASCADE *Books* • Eugene, Oregon

FAITH WITHOUT BELIEF
A Guide for Doubters

Cascade Books
An Imprint of Wipf and Stock Publishers
199 W. 8th Ave., Suite 3
Eugene, OR 97401

www.wipfandstock.com

PAPERBACK ISBN: 978-1-6667-8808-2
HARDCOVER ISBN: 978-1-6667-8809-9
EBOOK ISBN: 978-1-6667-8810-5

Cataloguing-in-Publication data:

Names: King, Derek S., author.

Title: Faith without belief : a guide for doubters / by Derek S. King.

Description: Eugene, OR: Cascade Books, 2024 | Includes bibliographical refer-
ences.

Identifiers: ISBN 978-1-6667-8808-2 (paperback) | ISBN 978-1-6667-8809-9
(hardcover) | ISBN 978-1-6667-8810-5 (ebook)

Subjects: LCSH: Hidden God. | Faith—Theology. | Belief and doubt—Religious
aspects—Christianity.

Classification: BT774 K50 2024 (paperback) | BT774 (ebook)

VERSION NUMBER 09/06/24

For Bethany

Contents

Introduction

"WE ALL NEED SOMEONE to believe in. Every child I have ever looked after has someone: an angel. You've got to have faith. You've got to believe." So said Maggie Nelson, when asked about her foster child's supernatural angel vision in the critically acclaimed *Angels in the Outfield* (1994). You see, Roger has a gift. He can see angels, but no one else can see them. That's not all. The angels are acting strange. The angels are conspiring to help an otherwise atrocious baseball team, the Angels, win baseball games. Roger's insistence, and the miracle that is the Angels winning, slowly convinces people that he can, in fact, see angels. Maggie's defense of Roger's gift is the thread running through the rest of the movie. What do we do when faced with the seemingly unbelievable? What does it mean to have faith and to believe?

Most of us aren't tempted to believe supernatural beings are backing an American League team to take them to the top. But we're faced, in one way or another, with belief in God. Whether we were raised religious or not, it's likely we've contemplated God at some point in our lives. You may find the idea of God repulsive or you may find it beautiful. For some of us, belief in God comes easy. Maybe we're raised in it and we never give serious thought to leaving it. But for some of us, belief doesn't come so easy. My friend Ben was raised with belief, but he still struggles to believe in God.[1]

---

1. Ben's story is a true story, but I changed his name at his request. A special

It's not for lack of wanting. He sees the appeal. Like many from the American Midwest, he grew up in and around church. Many of his friends are Christians. Beyond friends and family, he sees the church as a community of belonging. And community is a universal human longing. On top of these surface benefits, Ben finds much beauty in the Christian story. He *hopes* it's true. He wants to become a Christian. But there's this big, fat barrier: he's not sure it's true.

Ben is not the caricature of a college student taking his first philosophy class. He doesn't think Christianity is only for dunces. He knows some of the brightest minds in the history of the world have been Christians. He's read some of them. He counts Christian apologists like C. S. Lewis and G. K. Chesterton amongst his favorite authors. He enjoys a good late-night conversation about theology or the Bible. And he grants there are several strong arguments for God. It's not just pie-in-the-sky delusion. There are good reasons to believe. But accepting even the basic claims of Christianity is a big ask for an active and skeptical mind. Ben questions *everything*. He doubts *everything*. He wants to believe in God. But he simply finds it difficult to believe it all. And how can he give his life to something he doubts? What's Ben to do?

That simple question is the heart of this book: what can Ben do?

It's a simple question, but there's no easy answer. We're sometimes tempted into easy answers. Following Maggie's appeal, we're tempted to say, "Just believe." But this one-size-fits-all solution turns out not to deliver like we might hope. For one, it doesn't wrestle with the complexities of belief. As I write this sentence, I'm looking out a window from a coffee shop. I see a gym, a Chevy Tahoe, a tree, a stop sign, and a liquor store. Suppose you told me, "Stop believing that tree exists." Taking a sip of coffee with brow wrinkled, it'd take me a moment to even make sense of such a demand. Even if Jeff Bezos offered to back an Amazon truck filled with money and unload it in my driveway, I *couldn't* believe

---

thanks to Ben for agreeing to be featured in my book and allowing me to interview him.

there's no tree. I might *say* "there's no tree"—it's a lot of money, after all. But I'd be lying. That's one (goofy) example, but a lot of our beliefs work that way. I believe Jupiter and Australia exist. I've never been to either. I believe the black liquid in my mug came from beans, though I've never observed the process. These are all beliefs. But I didn't *choose* them. They simply happened. You can tell me "just believe" until you're blue in the face, but it wouldn't move the needle. You could throw all the threats and rewards in the world at me, and my beliefs wouldn't budge. We don't choose beliefs like they're cereal at the supermarket.

Of course, it's not so simple. It rarely is. Maybe some of our beliefs, like that Jupiter or coffee beans exist, are like that, but is belief in God really like that? Some of our beliefs just happen to us, but some are shaped by our desires. Don't believe me? Go to almost any sporting event and watch the fans of opposing teams when the referee makes a close call. Where I'm from, Kentucky basketball is a way of life. I don't think I've ever watched a game in which Kentucky lost and the referees did a good job. I'm not sure it's possible. The reason, of course, is that as fans we're primed to see what we want to see. We can't help but see a close call through that lens. That's an obvious way our desires shape our beliefs. But it can happen more subtly and indirectly, too. Even when we don't choose our beliefs like cereal from a supermarket, we do choose communities or contexts in which we're more likely to form the beliefs we want. If it's cereal you seek, you're more likely to walk out with a box of Fruit Loops when you confine your search to the sugary section and avoid the section with healthy granola. To take an example with beliefs, I have a, let's say, *strong* suspicion of conspiracy theories. But suppose I decided today that I'm diving into the deep end of online conspiracy theories. It may not be long before I find myself doubting the existence of Finland.[2] My future self may say, "Well, I didn't *choose* to believe that Finland doesn't exist." But that's not quite right. My choices clearly shaped my belief even if they aren't solely responsible for it. Still, even when

2. You can find defense of the view that Finland doesn't exist on the internet. But I've been to Helsinki, so it'd be a tough pill to swallow.

xi

I'm intentional about putting myself in certain situations or communities, there's no guarantee I'll form the beliefs I want to form. Beliefs can be fickle things. All this to say: Finland exists and it's very difficult to "just believe" anything.

This book is about Christian faith and belief. I'm a Christian. I believe the claims of Christianity are true. But I also harbor doubt from time to time. I'll go out on a limb and guess I'm not the only one. Even so, each person's experience with belief and doubt is different. I've worked in college ministry for more than ten years. That's how I met Ben, in fact. But I meet a lot of students like Ben. Since my time in this ministry, I fell into the reputation of the "apologetics guy." And what comes with such an illustrious title? It basically means that when students come to our staff or leaders with tough questions about the Bible or Jesus or God, they get sent my way. I don't mind. I love the conversations and it's given me a wider perspective on the questions students have and what's behind them. I've heard doubts that range from "[shoulder shrug] just curious" to "my faith is crumbling like a Jenga tower." It becomes clear quickly: everyone's doubts are different. What they all have in common is there's some nagging difficulty about believing in the basic claims of Christianity.

When I say the basic claims of Christianity, I mean the *basics*, like God created the world, humans sinned, Jesus is God in the body, he taught and performed miracles in and around Jerusalem in the first century, he was crucified and rose from the dead, and he ascended into heaven. You know, the greatest hits. For those of us who grew up in a Christian culture, we're almost numb to the story. But have you ever stepped back and thought about it? It's quite a story! It's at least understandable if many today are hesitant to bet their lives on the two-thousand-year-old stories of some uneducated fisherman. The problem is many of us think these beliefs *necessary* to be a Christian. You might even think being a Christian *just is* having these beliefs. That's *all it means* to be a Christian. You either have these beliefs or you don't. But what about those who struggle to believe? What about those of us with doubts? What about people like Ben?

Before we go further, let me say clearly what this book is *not*: this book doesn't try to convince you Christianity is true. Okay, I dabble in a bit of that in chapter 1. But I know the reasons to believe I all too briefly lay out in this chapter aren't likely to convince you. The goal, rather, is to show that Christianity is intellectually respectable. The beliefs *are* important, after all. Faith, whatever else it is, isn't necessarily *blind*. Though my purpose isn't to convince you, it's not because I think it's unimportant. But there are a lot of excellent resources out there already for that. This book sprouted from conversations with Ben. As someone deeply impacted by Christian apologetics, I'm always happy to discuss the objections to Christianity and reasons to believe. But it became clear from my conversations with Ben that "think harder" was about as viable a response to his questions as "just believe." Ben is sharp. He thinks longer and harder about God than almost every Christian I know. He knows the arguments and objections. But he still struggles to get there.

Who's this book for, then? It's for the nonbelievers and doubters among us. We'll get clear on those terms later but, in short, it's for people who struggle to believe in God or in Jesus. That includes folks in and out of the church. This book is for people who do and don't claim the title "Christian." Whether we call it "nonbelief" or "doubt," it's for people who think or feel the Christian story is not or may not be true, whether they want it to be true or not. We can all agree this kind of doubt is an enormous barrier to hurdle for faith in Jesus and Christian living. This book is about the hurdle. It's about what to do when you've tried and failed to believe. It's about what to do when you do believe . . . sometimes. It's about what to do when the doubts just won't go away. This book is about God's grace for nonbelievers and doubters—and what we can do in response.

Outline

If you're like me, you want to know what you're getting into before you start. Is this a movie about romance, action, horror, or angels helping a baseball team win? Starting a book is no different. A brief outline helps orient us to the path and let us know what we're getting into. It's especially important for books, which we might put down for a few hours, weeks, or—perish the thought!—months while reading. But you can always return here to remind yourself of the main points without getting lost in the weeds. To boil the argument of the book down to one simple point, it's this: Christian faith is more like trust than "belief" and faith is possible even when you feel stuck in nonbelief. That may sound obvious to some of you and scandalous to others. But I hope to show how faith without belief is possible and offer guidance for those with severe doubts about how to doubt wisely.

The first chapter is the *Reasonableness of Faith*. It may seem like an odd place to start to show "faith without belief" because this chapter argues Christian *belief* is on solid ground. An initial barrier to Christianity, for many, is the nasty myth that Christianity is intellectually bankrupt. In other words, Christianity is for dummies. And when you go to church, you check your brain at the door. But it is not so. There are many more extensive, excellent resources that lay out the case for Christianity better than I'll do here, but it's important to start with a case that Christianity is reasonable and worthy of our belief. I present some of the reasons to believe in God and the resurrection of Jesus that I find most compelling and respond (all too briefly) to some objections against God's existence. I'm under no illusions that these arguments will convince everyone—we wouldn't need the rest of the book, if that were the case! But I hope, at least, to show that Christianity isn't just for fools and faith isn't blind.

Chapter 2 is *Why We Doubt Anyway*. Despite a strong intellectual case in favor of Christianity, many of us harbor significant doubt anyway. We could compile a long list of reasons for this. But this chapter will focus on two reasons, one unchanging and one contemporary: the effects of sin and secularity. Sin has been around *almost* as long as humanity itself. But we too often ignore its role in shaping our habits of mind, including our belief in God. Apart from how sin shapes our beliefs, we live in a world that teaches us to doubt. Modern cultural forces beyond our individual defects shape us into nonbelievers. We live in what some have called "a secular age." Unlike our ancestors, belief in God or the supernatural doesn't come natural to us. We'll explore how this shapes and invites our doubts.

Chapter 3 is *Help Thou My Unbelief: Faith without Belief*. This is my case for faith without belief, in a six thousand-ish word nutshell. Using a story from the Gospel and an analogy of arranged marriages, I argue severe doubt or nonbelief is *not* an insurmountable barrier for faith. While we often equate Christianity with accepting certain propositions as true, the central movement of the Christian faith is *faith* or *trust*. That's not to say the beliefs are irrelevant. They aren't. But faith is less like saying "this is true" and more like a commitment to a way of living. Because of this, faith is compatible with doubt—even a significant degree of doubt. Even so, faith must latch onto *something*. I suggest faith can latch onto hope. We can hope that God is up to something even if we struggle to accept beliefs about him.

Chapter 4 is *Christian Living for Nonbelievers*. It sounds counterintuitive, I know. But faith without belief is *Christian* faith. It's a commitment to Jesus Christ, his teaching, and his church. But even if we grant the compatibility of faith and doubt, there's the awkward business of Christian living: how then should a nonbeliever live in faith? Christian living includes important spiritual disciplines or practices, Scripture-reading and prayer among them. In addition to these practices, however, Christian living is in community. It's especially so for nonbelievers. The church can be a lifeline for our beliefs. In a short *Conclusion*, I offer final reflections on belief. But I'd especially encourage you to see the *Further Reading* section after the conclusion. I offer some recommendations for books on (or near) theme if you want to go further. I can't answer all the questions in such a short book and I can't help thinking about the questions left unexplored. The *Further Reading* section gives you a way to explore these questions.

Two final things I hope go without saying, but, in case they don't, I'll say them anyway. First, Christian beliefs are important.

The basic claims of Christianity are not mere propositions. They are *true* and communicate the message of salvation for the world. My emphasis on faith in this book should not be taken as a dismissal of belief. Second, in this book, I suggest one way forward for a nonbeliever. But it is *one* way. I've heard powerful conversion stories that credit huge roles to apologetics, beautiful art, participation in a Christian community, or even overt divine manifestations. People see or experience God in a myriad of ways. Many of those ways lead to explicit belief. Thanks be to God that it is so! But everyone's story is different. The path I propose is not the path for everyone. But it is the path for some. For those, I pray for a lamp to their feet and a light for their path.

1

Faith Isn't Blind

The Reasonableness
of Christianity

*"Innumerable forces are vying for the future, and
Christianity may prove considerably weaker than its
rivals. This should certainly be no cause of despair
for Christians, however, since they must believe their
faith to be not only a cultural logic but a cosmic
truth, which can never finally be defeated."*

—DAVID BENTLEY HART, *ATHEIST DELUSIONS*

BELIEVE IT OR NOT, college is not about beer. It's a good time
for meeting people, sharing different experiences, and engaging
new ideas. It's a time for *questions*. College classes should invite
them. But even when they don't, it's difficult to avoid. Going to
college is like being a stuffed animal plucked by a claw crane and
dropped into a new home. I remember the day my parents moved
me to Lexington, Kentucky, a two-hour drive from the small, ru-
ral community in which I grew up. There are few moments in
life I remember so vividly as laying in my bed the first night in

Lexington, mulling the fact that my world had just been slapped off its tilt. The next time I went "home," I'd be there as a guest. I was in Lexington to attend the University of Kentucky, but the far more pressing education was learning independence. I had to learn how to do laundry. How to make soup. And how to keep a schedule. Things that now seem laughably simple were daunting new tasks overshadowed only by the fact that I knew my life would never be the same. My life was no longer being laid out for me like tomorrow's clothes. It was all on me now. The laundry and the soup came easy. What needed ironing out were the important things: What are my values? What do I believe?

In the middle of all this, I came across a C. S. Lewis quote: "Christianity, if false, is of no importance, and if true, of infinite importance. The only thing it cannot be is moderately important."[1] I grew up in church. I was a YPK—a youth pastor's kid. That meant church twice on Sunday and once on Wednesday. That meant summer camp and retreats. Christian living *was* important to me. But, until I read that quote, I didn't realize it was only moderately important. I went to church (most weeks) and read my Bible (most days), but Christianity was more like an appendage on my life rather than its beating heart. The Lewis quote hit me hard. I knew he was right. But then I read the quote again (and again). The quote isn't just about whether Christianity is important to me. It's about whether Christianity *is true*.

Like fabric softener, I'd never thought of that before. Christianity was almost too essential for me to question it. I'm sure it wasn't Lewis's intention, but that's what I did: I questioned it. I started to ask questions and read objections. Many of these objections were new to me. I made a habit of—kids, don't try this at home—watching online debates about God's existence and fast-forwarding through the Christian parts. If there were strong objections to Christianity, I wanted to hear them. And, I know this is going to be hard to believe but, guess what? I started to have doubts. I wondered whether it was true after all. Faced with Lewis's quote, I feared giving my life to something that wasn't true. I didn't

---

1. Lewis, *God in the Dock*, 102.

want to be hoodwinked by the promise of God, especially since it all sounded so good—almost *too* good. I harvested questions and objections like berries in a basket. But then began the search for answers. And, to my surprise, I found answers—*a lot* of answers. Some of these answers were bad answers. But some, I thought, were good answers. Some were *really* good. I was bowled over with the level of thought and sophistication displayed in the case for God. Christianity was no longer only appealing or how I was raised. It started to *make sense*. My faith was never, and is not now, about making sense of God—as if such a thing is even possible. But there was, still, a great comfort when I realized that belief in God didn't require me to check my brain at the door.

In this chapter, I want to pass along some of the reasons for faith I find compelling. I can't reproduce, in one short chapter, the breadth or depth of arguments for God's existence. Not only are there several different arguments for God's existence, but many of these arguments have long histories. They've been developed with rigor by theologians and philosophers much more intelligent than I. For those well versed in the arguments, my presentations here will seem trite and incomplete—because they are. But my goal isn't to hash the arguments to completion. My case isn't comprehensive. All I want to do is lay out reasons for faith I find compelling in the hopes you'll see Christian belief as a reasonable option. While my faith has strengthened considerably in the many years since this period of doubt, I'm not immune from doubt. These arguments are like vaccinations. They don't guarantee you'll be doubt-free and their force usually wears off after awhile. But they're important to revisit for that reason: they remind us faith isn't empty or a blind leap. The three reasons for faith I present here remain, to this day, masts to which I latch myself when the luring songs of doubt stick in my head. That's why I want to start here. Although I'll make the case that faith is compatible with doubt, faith is more difficult when it's aimed at something we deem silly or incredible.

Christian belief is a lot easier to swallow when you believe God exists and Jesus rose from the dead. The reasons for belief I find most compelling, then, are aimed in those directions. The three I'll explore in this chapter are simply (1) the universe began, (2) good exists, and (3) Jesus rose from the dead. Together, they make, I think, a powerful case for the reasonableness of faith. I'll look at each in turn and show why I think it's a compelling reason to believe.

The Universe Began

For those who don't know him, Carl Sagan was like a 1980s Bill Nye but with better degrees. Astrophysicists normally aren't famous, but Sagan was the closest an astrophysicist gets to the Beatles thanks to his television program *Cosmos*.[2] This thirteen-part PBS series was one of the most-watched programs at the time and introduced viewers, at an accessible level, to the vastness of our universe. Sagan taught a whole generation about our solar system and beyond, buttressed by technological innovations in astronomy. The opening shot of the entire program is Sagan walking out on a stunning, green cliffside with enormous waves crashing in behind him. The baritone timbre of his voice rings out with authority, "The cosmos is all that is or was or ever will be." It's quite an opening!

Sagan has the natural air of authority. But even if he didn't, you want to listen to an accomplished scientist talking about the cosmos. His knowledge of the universe is almost as vast as the universe itself. But, unfortunately, he seems not to realize his opening line isn't about the cosmos at all. Neither, in fact, is it scientific. Sagan's claim is not about what he's observed but what he can't observe. It's not about the cosmos, but what's *beyond* it. Among other things, he implies God doesn't exist. God, after all, isn't part of the cosmos. If the cosmos is "all that is," then he leaves no room for God. But how could such a claim be scientific? Isn't science empirically verifiable? Doesn't it study the *natural* world? Sagan begins his scientific program with a claim that's anything but

---

2. Carl Sagan, *Cosmos*, PBS.

scientific. You can't investigate what's beyond the cosmos with a telescope. That's a claim for philosophy.

Thankfully, philosophers are on the case (is that the first time anyone's ever said this?). For as long as there've been philosophers, philosophers have thought long and hard about the universe and our place in it. In fact, the very existence of our universe—that there is *something* rather than *nothing*—is often seen as evidence for God. The argument for God's existence based on the cosmos is appropriately named the "cosmological argument." Perhaps the most famous version of the cosmological argument comes from the medieval biblical scholar-philosopher-theologian Thomas Aquinas. If you have a question about God, I'll bet all the money in my pocket (which, to be fair, isn't much) Aquinas answered it. You may not always like his answer, but you can't say he didn't think about it. Every year, college freshmen in Philosophy 101 courses are introduced to his "Five Ways."[3] The Five Ways are the ways Aquinas thinks we can prove God exists. He starts with an observation about our world and reasons from there.

The first three ways work with a similar idea. They look at chains of "motion" or "causes." So, for example, Thomas will say something super obvious: things are in motion or things have causes. Okay, we're tracking. Then, he takes another step: causes and effects form a sort of chain. This cause was caused by this cause and so on and so on. So, I moved my arm to touch my head because my brain told my arm to do so, but my brain told my arm to do so because I needed an example of cause and effect, and I needed an example of cause of effect because I'm writing this book, and I'm writing this book because blah blah blah and so on. Or it may be easier to think of this chain of causes like a family tree. I'm the son of Doug, Doug is the son of Thomas, and on and on it goes. That's a chain of causes. So far, so good?

Then, Aquinas takes a further step. He says we can take any chain of causes and follow each link back really, really, *really* far. *But*, and here's the key point, the chain can't go on *forever*. You can trace your ancestry back a long way but, eventually, you know, you hit,

3. Thomas Aquinas, *Summa Theologiae*, I.2.3.

like, Adam and Eve. The chain stops *somewhere*. That makes sense, right? Well, Aquinas says this is true of *any* chain of physical causes. The chain *can't* stretch into infinity because infinity isn't a real number. We're getting into theory of theory, but it's a rather simple idea. What's infinity plus one? You can't add one to infinity and get a new, higher number. But in any chain of causes, we're adding one all the time. The chain isn't infinite. We could, in theory, trace any chain back and find a beginning. I don't care what a cartoon in a spacesuit told you, there is no "infinity and beyond."

If we're still tracking with Aquinas, we can say, then, that for any chain of causes, there's a beginning. There's a *first* cause. But, wait a minute, where'd that cause come from? Who caused the beginning? Aquinas, who fawns over Aristotle like a teenage girl at a Taylor Swift concert, follows Aristotle in his conclusion: there must be an "uncaused causer." It's the only rational conclusion. There must be something that is itself *uncaused* but which *can* cause. To put it another way, the dominos only fall if someone flicks the first domino. Now, it also stands to reason the first domino doesn't flick itself. Whatever this "uncaused causer" is, it must stand outside the chain. It simply exists, in and of itself. But it puts all else into motion. And this, concludes Aquinas, we call God.

Okay, maybe all this talk is giving you motion sickness. Let's simplify things a bit. The basic idea is more straightforward: when we see something, we know it came from somewhere. It didn't just pop into existence. Consider the mysterious case of the NYC Burger.[4] In 2019, Lincoln Boehm was walking down the streets of Queens, in New York City, at 6:30 AM when he stumbled upon something that "genuinely shook me to my core." What he found was a perfectly wrapped burger from the popular restaurant chain In-N-Out. Okay, so someone threw their trash on the street in NYC—what's news about that? What shook Boehm was the fact that In-N-Out doesn't have a location east of the Mississippi River. The closest In-N-Out was thousands of miles away. Boehm happened

---

4. https://nypost.com/2019/07/21/mysterious-untouched-in-n-out-burger-found-lying-on-queens-street/. Thanks to C. J. Carter, who unknowingly gave me the idea for this story.

to be an In-N-Out enthusiast and knew it wasn't a wolf (a McDonald's burger) in sheep's clothing (an In-N-Out wrapper). The burger was authentic. This was the real deal. The question was: how'd it get there? When Boehm posted the picture online, there were a lot of theories. Internet commenters were on the case. Boehm's leading theory was a rich person woke up on the West Coast, loaded up on In-N-Out burgers, flew to NYC in a private jet, then started tossing them out the window as a joke. Hey, can you do better? But, notably, no one seriously proposed the burger just came out of nowhere. There must've been *some* explanation.[5]

The inference to God kind of works like our inference that the burger got to NYC somehow. It didn't just pop into existence out of nothing and from nothing, right? *Right*? Well, some people don't think so. Lawrence Krauss, for example, argues the universe came from "nothing."[6] That sure would simplify things, wouldn't it? There's nothing—nothing at all—then—poof!—there's something. And he thinks he's got the science to prove it. There's only one problem: it's nonsense. It turns out Krauss doesn't deliver on his promise. Because there's one tiny hitch in his plan: he's smuggled in all sorts of somethings into his definition of nothing. He admits as much. He says, "For surely 'nothing' is every bit as physical as 'something.'" It turns out, what he means by "nothing" is a "quantum vacuum" or "empty space," both subjects to a string of physical laws—literally, *physics*. It gets better. He dismisses what "philosophers mean by nothing" and adds the cherry on top, "I care about the 'nothing' of reality. And if the 'nothing' of reality is full of stuff, then I'll go with that."[7]

Wait, what? Rewind. According to Krauss, "nothing" is both "physical" and "full of stuff"? If that's head scratching to you, you're not alone. Krauss's attempt to prove the universe came from

---

5. Unfortunately, it was not conclusive evidence God exists and had a rather ordinary explanation. https://nypost.com/2019/07/24/how-mystery-in-n-out-burger-wound-up-on-a-queens-street/#.

6. Krauss, *Universe from Nothing*.

7. https://www.theatlantic.com/technology/archive/2012/04/has-physics-made-philosophy-and-religion-obsolete/256203/.

nothing amounts to the radical thesis that the universe came from physical stuff—or what we sometimes call "something." Krauss *desperately* wants to explain the universe and all its causes from the inside. He wants the universe to explain itself. But the explanation can't come from the inside any more than Tiny Tim can be the author of *A Christmas Carol*. Krauss runs, face first, into the very problem Aquinas and Aristotle were getting at. Where'd that "stuff" that Krauss so dubiously calls "nothing" come from? And on and on it goes. The universe *began*. But how?

Now comes the obvious question: "Okay big shot: you're telling me God is the cause of everything but who caused God?" Remember, first, that Aquinas and Aristotle want to say the logical conclusion of the chain is there must be an "uncaused causer." *Something* must be uncaused, but what is it? Aquinas adds "this we call God" because God is uncaused. For Aquinas, to ask "who caused God?" is a category mistake. It's an absurd question, on par with "who is the bachelor's spouse?" or "how long is the fourth side of that triangle?" The uncaused causer is, by definition, *uncaused*. To put it in those terms, the question turns out to be: "who caused that which is uncaused?" God simply *is* and always has been. Many traditional theologians have even been hesitant to say "God exists" because that falsely suggests God exists like you and I exist. God doesn't just "exist," he's the ground and source of all existence itself. He stands outside of time and space and is not constrained by them. For these reasons, God is a good candidate for the "uncaused causer." Without that first and final explanation, we're left with an infinite chain of causes and that simply won't do.

It should be obvious by now, but we've not arrived at the Christian God. We can't say, "the universe began to exist, therefore Jesus rose from the dead." But from the fact that the universe began, we can reason to an uncaused causer. I warned you at the beginning these reasons would be introductory in nature. There's a lot more we could say, including scientific reasons to think the universe had a beginning or reasons to think infinity isn't a real, ever-increasing number. But what compels me is more basic and intuitive. It's simply: The universe began, but how? God seems like the best explanation.

Good Exists

Godwin's Law is something of an internet meme. The law states that the longer online discussion about a topic continues, the probability of someone making a comparison to Hitler or the Nazis approaches 100 percent. If you've spent much time in comment sections or online forums, you see why it's called a "law." The other day I was reading an article about baseball and someone was compared to Hitler in the comment section. Imagine the articles about politics (or don't for your own sanity). How does it always come to this? The Nazis are everyone's favorite comparison. But there's a good reason why people jump to Nazi comparisons: the Nazis are a *universal* symbol of evil. Few examples work anymore because we rarely share the same moral intuitions. But right or left, religious or nonreligious, rich or poor, we can all agree the Nazis were bad. Hitler is humanity's arch villain. The sheer scale and horror of Hitler's reign and terror may be unmatched in human history, which is absolutely saying something!

I'll try to avoid comparing anyone to Hitler. Godwin's Law doesn't apply to books. But Hitler is at least useful for this thought experiment. Imagine, for a moment, the worst outcome of World War II: the Nazis not only win the war and conquer Europe, but they eventually march on the rest of the world, too. In his final solution to the problem of non-Nazis, Hitler murders everyone in the world who disagrees with him. In this awful and terrifying scenario, the only people left in the world are Nazis. Every living human is pro-Hitler and thinks he's a genius hero. Now that's a bleak situation. This is Cormac McCarthy on steroids. Here's the question: In this scenario, is Hitler morally good?

It may sound like a stupid question. No, it *is* a stupid question. But morality thought experiments thrive on stupid questions. The goal of a thought experiment like this is to expose our moral intuitions. It's meant to show how we *instinctively* think about good and evil. So it's telling that, when presented with the scenario and asked if Hitler is morally good, we want to scream, *"No, of course not!"* Hitler is still a moral monster, even if everyone on earth disagrees. But notice what such an answer tells us about morality. It tells us we don't think morality depends on what we humans *think* about morality. In the thought experiment, 100 percent of people in the world think Hitler is morally good. But that doesn't matter to us. Most of us probably don't even consider it when answering the question. And while that's especially evident in this scenario, it typically holds true of how we think of the moral issues of our day, too. When we ask if an action or policy is morally good or bad, we don't ask for a show of hands. Morality transcends human opinion about what is right or wrong.

Because morality is not subject to human opinion and presents us with a way we ought to behave, we call it a moral law. The moral law is just a set of regulations that determine whether actions are good or bad. Helping an old lady cross the street? Good. Tripping her with her cane? Bad. Baking a pie for your neighbor? Good. Lacing it with arsenic? Bad. Some actions are good or bad—irrevocably, always, no matter who's doing them or when.[8] But the much trickier question is *why* are some acts right and some acts wrong? Hitler must've had a tortured conscience. But, at the same time, he was motivated by what he *thought* was right. He believed in ideas. He had a vision for what he deemed good. But *why* doesn't Hitler get to decide what's right and wrong? Who's to tell him murder is bad? We've already agreed we can't put it to a vote. What makes a moral a *law*?

To try to answer these questions, we might reach for natural explanations. Maybe a moral sense evolved in us over millions of years and that explains morality. Maybe a "herd instinct" evolved in us to help us survive. So now we care about other humans, even when they're not part of our tribe. This might explain altruistic

8. I can't resist further clarification: *of course*, most actions are only good or bad depending on the context. If your neighbor is a mass murderer and you're lacing the pie with arsenic to save lives, the moral waters get considerably murkier.

actions, like a solider diving on a grenade to save his comrades—
or even unknown civilians. But natural explanations don't get us
very far. Such explanations might explain the existence of some
moral laws, but they can't explain why we should follow them. Put
another way: even if evolution could explain why we think mur-
dering our neighbor with an arsenic-laced pie is wrong, it can't
tell us we shouldn't do it. Why should I feel guilt over it if it's only
wrong because of physical mutations in a brain millions of years
ago? After all, we transgress the bounds of our evolution all the
time. Just because a desire naturally occurs in our brains doesn't
mean we should follow it or following it is morally permissible.
Natural explanations can tell an origin story for morality. But it
can't tell us we ought to behave in certain ways.

For moral obligations, we need something more stable. We
need something, or someone, who exists completely independent
of human beings, who has an interest in good, and who compels
us to behave in accordance with the moral law. To borrow a phrase
from Aquinas: this, we call God. God is the best explanation for
the moral law. Without God, it's difficult to see how the moral law
could exist. This position is often misunderstood. I'm *not* saying
people can't know right and wrong without the Bible or religion.
Clearly, non-Christians have some recognition of the moral law,
too. An atheist knows he shouldn't put arsenic in the pie even if
he hasn't read the Ten Commandments. Sure, there may be some
differences in what we count as right or wrong, but we all—all humans and all cultures—recognize *good exists*. Not only that, but
we agree we should pursue good things. We should do good and
not evil. But for good to have the kind of universality we imagine
it to have, it must be anchored somewhere outside of ourselves.
Otherwise, it's adrift at sea. Religious folk have always found God
a suitable anchor. If God exists, it's reasonable to think good has
a fixed point apart from what we humans think about the good.
It also adds a layer of meaning to our actions, which take on an
eternal flavor. But if God doesn't exist, it's difficult to see why we
should care about doing right or wrong. Let's eat, drink, and be

merry however we see fit, because in a few million years the earth will melt and nothing will matter.

Since we've taken a dark turn, let's descend deeper and consider a problem with anchoring good in God. Good exists, yes—but so does evil. Many are (rightly) troubled by the vast amount of suffering, pain, and evil in our world. If the cosmos is all there is, so be it—it's the hand we're dealt, and we must play it. But evil seems like a problem for the existence of a good and loving God. The so-called problem of evil asks: If there is a good and loving God who can stop evil and unnecessary suffering, why doesn't he? Answers to this question don't come easy, nor should they. Answers to the problem of evil often feel flat, but for good reason. Evil feels wrong because it *is* wrong. Things aren't the way God intended them to be. Evil is, literally, *absurd*. It doesn't belong in God's good, created order. Recognizing this, the Christian tradition has held that evil doesn't exist in and of itself. Rather, everything is created good and we only experience evil when good things are distorted. Evil is nothing but the perversion of God's good order. So, there's something wrong about fitting it into God's good creation through nice, neat answers to the problem of evil. We literally cannot make sense of evil. It's senseless.

That doesn't mean, however, we can only throw up our hands and conclude God's a fraud. "God" as a general, catch-all term is insufficient, anyway. The story God tells about creation begins with the goodness of creation. God's story doesn't evade questions of evil, but places them within God's wider, redemptive narrative. Imagine watching Darth Vader say "I am your father" to Luke Skywalker without the context of the rest of the story. Without the wider narrative, it's hard to recognize the significance of any moment. But the story helps illuminate our darkness. When God made humans "very good," he made us image bearers. We share in God's own image. We're charged to rule like God rules, to bring order, to tend the land, and to reproduce. But things go awry—quickly. Humans disobey God's only command and, in doing so, throw God's good order into disorder. G. K. Chesterton says of creation, "God had written, not so much a poem, but rather a play; a play he had planned as perfect, but which had necessarily been left to human actors and stage-managers, who had since made a great mess of it."[9]

In God's great mercy, he still wants us to be part of his play. But the play is now about our redemption and the redemption of the rest of creation. Our central role is now to tell God's story and invite the whole of creation into proper relationship with God and others. Like our responsibility at creation, that's a big role with gargantuan effects. We still get it wrong, a lot, and the result of our disobedience can be evil. But even if, in the short term, our disobedience can separate creation or ourselves from God, we can rest knowing God has taken ultimate responsibility. He uses our stuttering, forgotten lines, and overacting to make a beautiful play, anyway. Even our failed attempts at good will be reworked by the cosmic playwright. He's promised to set things completely right and bring our disorder back into order. He's promised to defeat evil and make things *good* again.

We can't sweep evil under the rug. Pain and suffering hurt. They're parts of our deeply broken creation. In God's redemption story, the victorious battle is won but we await its ultimate fulfillment. Theologians like to talk about the "already . . . but not yet." A favorite analogy is we live between D-Day and VE Day: the decisive battle (D-Day) is over, but the war rages on toward its inevitable end (VE Day). God is not only the only suitable anchor for good. He is our only *hope* for good. The reason we feel the problem of evil so strongly, after all, is because God made us for his goodness. That's why we feel moral responsibility and the brokenness of the world. We feel—we *know*—we're made for good. C. S. Lewis, reflecting on his own doubts as an atheist, recognized his argument against God depended on an ultimate anchor for goodness he couldn't provide. He reflected on this like so:

> My argument against God was that the universe seemed so cruel and unjust. But how had I got this idea of just and unjust? A man does not call a line crooked unless he has some idea of a straight line. What was I comparing

9. Chesterton, *Orthodoxy*, 84.

this universe with when I called it unjust? If the whole show was bad and senseless from A to Z, so to speak, why did I, who was supposed to be part of the show, find myself in such a violent reaction against it? . . . If the whole universe has no meaning, we should never have found out that it has no meaning: just as, if there were no light in the universe and therefore no creatures with eyes, we should never have known it was dark. Dark would be without meaning.[10]

Between the "already . . . but not yet" we experience the wicked effects of the fall. Pain and deep suffering are still with us until the final consummation of God's redemption plan. But the intellectual argument from evil loses its fangs when it depends on an ultimate, unchanging standard for what's good or just. That's a standard only God can provide.

So, good exists—independent of us—and this gives us a powerful reason to think God exists, too. If there's a moral law, there's a law giver. The creation of the universe and our obligation to the moral law are central to God's story. But many see the story as just that: a story. A beautiful story, maybe, but no truer than *Peter Rabbit* or *Alice in Wonderland*. And yet, unlike any other religion, Christianity has the audacity to claim its God—the maker of heaven and earth who is himself outside of heaven and earth—also entered it. The fulcrum of Christian faith is not arguments about God's existence. It's a historical event. It's something that happened in our time and space and is, in principle, verifiable and falsifiable. Other religions can't say the same. No one can *prove*, without a shadow of doubt, Joseph Smith or Muhammad, for example, *didn't* have divine revelations. We must take their word for it (if we're so inclined). But Christianity is different. The bones of Jesus are a defeater for Christianity. The apostle Paul said as much when he said, "If Christ is not raised, your faith is useless" (1 Corinthians 15:14). Faith stands or falls on this event. The question is: did it happen?

10. Lewis, *Mere Christianity*, 38–39.

Jesus Rose from the Dead

Cleopatra was an Egyptian queen. Julius Caesar crossed the Rubicon. In the Middle Ages, chess evolved in India and a plague ravished Europe. George Washington was the first president of the USA. George Washington Carver did wonders with peanuts. Jane Austen wrote brilliant novels and Stephen F. Austin did something in Texas. Bill Gates and Steve Jobs shaped the way we interact with our world. People, events, places—these make up a long, long timeline we call history. History stretches back as far as we can trace and to every traceable corner of the globe. When we study history, we learn about the past. We might learn about seminal moments that lead to our present moment (see: the industrial revolution). Or we might learn about an obscure character who lived an interesting life (see: Moe Berg). But when we read history, we're reading an account of what happened.

Of course, that doesn't mean the account is perfect. Until we find the key that unlocks time travel, we're confined to learn about history from others. We can only read someone else's account. If we want to read firsthand accounts of the War for American Independence, we'll struggle to find an unbiased author. You can bet an American colonist and a British loyalist will have different takes. But they're both writing history. Even if they're writing from their own perspectives, they're telling a story that happened. They might embellish or exaggerate. They might conveniently leave details out. They might shape the narrative to suit their ends. But they are still trying to communicate, to anyone who'll read it, what happened. And, for whatever reason, they think what happened is worth recording.

Maybe because he often gets lumped in with other religious figures or gods, few seem to appreciate how much historical information we have about Jesus. Like another sage, Socrates, Jesus himself never wrote anything down, as far as we know. All we have are accounts by others about his life. Some of those are intimate, firsthand, eyewitness accounts (like the Gospels).[11] Others are from

11. To be precise, only the Gospels of Matthew and John are written by

later followers (like Paul's letters). Some are from non-Christian, Roman historians (like Tacitus and Seutonius). Others are from Jewish historians (like Josephus). For an ancient figure who lived mostly in an obscure corner of the Roman Empire, there's an astounding amount about Jesus in our historical record. But the best historical record about Jesus is the New Testament.

An objector might worry about this starting point. Since I'm trying to give reasons to believe, especially for those who struggle to believe, "the Bible tells me so" probably isn't going to be compelling for many people. "Yes," we can hear someone saying, "the Bible says Jesus rose from the dead, but what if I don't accept the Bible as God's word?" Fair enough. We can set aside the Christian assumption that the Bible is God's word, however, without setting aside the Bible. Whatever else it may be, the Bible is a collection of historical documents, too. These writings are written in by particular people, in a particular context, about particular events. Even as a purely historical exercise, we can't ask about Jesus and discard the New Testament. Put simply, from a historical perspective the New Testament includes the most important information about who Jesus was and what he did. The Gospels and letters contain eyewitness testimony and they're written relatively close to the events in question (especially by ancient standards). We don't need to litigate the historical reliability of every New Testament book, but it's important to see that, historically speaking, the New Testament is the most reliable source for Jesus we have.

Christianity doesn't stand or fall, however, on the reliability of the Bible. It stands or falls on the resurrection. If Christ is not raised, our faith is useless. You don't need the Bible to be saved—even if it helps *a lot*. An illiterate man is saved by his faith in Jesus Christ like the rest of us. But that faith must be in the man who claimed to be God and rose from the dead. The Gospels record Jesus's resurrection. But you don't need to be a dyed in the wool atheist to find the resurrection an incredible claim. After all, dead people usually stay dead. It's not unreasonable to want more.

---

confirmed eyewitnesses. But most scholars think Mark and Luke leaned heavily on apostolic, eyewitness testimony.

We could get into historical weeds here but let's not, okay? Apart from the direct testimony of the Gospels, we have solid historical reasons (many of them from non-Christian sources) for Jesus's crucifixion on a Roman cross, his empty tomb, conversions by skeptics, and hundreds of eyewitnesses to Jesus's resurrection. But I want to focus in on only one historical point: Jesus's followers really *believed* he'd risen from the dead.

The best reason, perhaps, for thinking that his followers believed he'd risen is that they died for it. The apostles didn't get money, sex, or fame from their story—you know, those things which typically motivate humans. Quite the opposite. They were ostracized, beaten, and killed for their message. Of course, just because you die for a message doesn't make it true. On September 11, the terrorists who flew planes into iconic US buildings surely *believed* that for which they died—but that doesn't make them right. It doesn't mean their beliefs were true. But surely they *believed* in their cause. The same is true of Jesus's disciples. For what it's worth, modern, non-Christian historians agree. Pointedly, agnostic scholar Bart Ehrman says, "It is a historical fact that some of Jesus' followers came to believe that he had been raised from the dead soon after his execution."[12] E. P. Sanders likewise says, "That Jesus' followers (and later Paul) had resurrection experiences is, in my judgment, a fact. What the reality was that gave rise to the experiences I do not know."[13] That's really the question, isn't it? What was the reality that gave rise to these resurrection experiences? What made the disciples so convinced Jesus had risen they were willing to die for him?

The game is afoot! History is sometimes like solving a crime. We can collect all the data we can get our hands on, but we often need an explanation for the data. We're like Benoit Blanc, surveying his crime scene, with an enormous hole at the center of all these historical facts—to quote Blanc, "a doughnut hole in the doughnut's hole," perhaps. The scene is spread out before us: the disciples, the men who'd spent every day with Jesus for years,

---

12. Ehrman, *New Testament*, 224.

13. Sanders, *Historical Figure of Jesus*, 280.

were so convinced Jesus resurrected they were willing to die for him. Why? Several explanations have been offered. The so-called "swoon theory," for example, takes a stab at it: Jesus never died. It goes something like this: Jesus only *appeared* to die on the cross, somehow survived, and later woke up in his tomb. His disciples, convinced he'd died, were stunned when they saw him only days later and concluded he must have risen again. It makes perfect sense! Except it doesn't. Even if you could believe that Jesus survived crucifixion (the Romans were pretty good at killing guys, no?), the recently crucified Jesus would surely need months' worth of medical attention to recover to full health. He'd be lucky to walk again. But he somehow hoodwinked these people he'd spent every day for the last few years with, only days later, into thinking he'd died and rose again? "Ignore the lash marks and bruises—nothing to see here!" That's a tough doughnut hole to swallow.

Alternative, natural explanations also fall flat. What if the disciples had a mass hallucination? That's something, I guess, but mass hallucinations are somewhere on the spectrum of extremely rare to impossible and it doesn't explain how many eyewitnesses, in different times and places, encountered the risen Jesus. What if the legend grew over time or it was a conspiracy by the apostles? We're back to that nagging fact that the disciples *really believed* Jesus died, and died for this message. They'd have virtually no motivation to conspire, and it led then to horrible places. And not *one* recanted. What if aliens did it? Tough to disprove that one. What if, what if, what if?

There are a lot of "What-ifs." But as far as I can tell, none of them offer a plausible alternative explanation for what we know about Jesus's death and his disciple's proclamation of his resurrection. "Well, hold on a minute," an objector might interject. "Maybe these are far-fetched theories, but could they really be more far-fetched than a dead man rose from the dead?" A resurrection, after all, isn't easy to believe! But why not? The question of whether a resurrection is plausible to us or not depends in part on whether we believe there is a God who can work miracles. Once you get there, a resurrection—even if rare or unlikely—is not an absurd explanation. Even if we're undecided on the question of God, we can't rule out the possibility of a miracle from the get-go. That's bringing a philosophical prejudice to the historical data. Further still, a resurrection is more plausible in the wider framework of God's redemption story. Jesus claimed to be the Jewish Messiah, the promised savior who would claim the decisive victory against the enemies of the Jews. Not only that, but Jesus made many claims that suggest he is divine, such as when he said, "Before Abraham was, I Am!" (John 8:58). He predicted his own death and resurrection. In view of all this, and the belief that God exists and can work miracles, Jesus's resurrection is the best explanation for the historical data.

It's true, of course, that dead people don't usually rise from the dead. But it's not like that was news to Jesus's disciples. In an act of what C. S. Lewis calls "chronological snobbery," we're tempted to look on these uneducated fisherman as unreliable narrators. "Oh, if they only knew about modern science, then they'd know dead people can't rise from the dead." The absurdity of this needs no more comment. The disciples knew how radical their message was, but they believed it, anyway. They didn't merely think or hope it was true, they knew it. Taking their words for it, we have good *historical* reasons to conclude Jesus rose from the dead. We're not asked simply to take one dude's word for it. The New Testament literally records *hundreds* of eyewitnesses. In lieu of a better explanation, this one seems like the best.

I can't emphasize this enough: my presentation of these reasons to believe is piecemeal and introductory at best. You can pick any one of these topics, read a book a week on it, and still never finish all the books on the topic before you die. But these reasons were and are compelling to me. More importantly, I hope they show Christian belief is not a blind leap in the dark. Faith never is, really. When we have faith in something, anything, we always have our reasons. Why have faith in this but not that? We're not simply rolling the dice or spinning a bottle. We have our reasons and Christian faith is no different. It's based on philosophical, moral, and historical evidence. And yet Christian faith is not merely a response to evidence. My personal experience with the risen Jesus is far more important than any argument or historical fact. But the important point here is that my experience doesn't require me to check my brain at the church door. I don't need to avoid thinking to believe or to have faith. These reasons, among others, simply show my faith is reasonable. And that's enough.

A Final Comfort

Several years ago, the campus ministry I attended welcomed one of the world's leading theologians to campus. I'll let him remain anonymous. I hadn't yet embarked on my theological studies but my interest in theology was growing. So I was excited to hear him. Now, I'm no genius now and I certainly wasn't at the time. But I made good grades and considered myself reasonably intelligent. I usually don't feel completely out of my league in conversations about subjects that interest me. But on this night, I was out of my league. I'm not even sure we were playing the same sport. It turns out this theologian, bright though he is, wasn't—how to put this?—the charismatic, engaging speaker normally required to keep the attention of college students. He basically read an academic theology paper to a crowd who'd do well to name the four Gospels. Most of the students hated it. It's lived on in the collective memory of our ministry as a laughable swing-and-miss. Along with the rest of the students, I watched as his lecture flew well over my head. But, even though I couldn't tell you what he talked about (I remember him mentioning Peter at one point), something did stick with me about that night. This guy was an intellectual heavyweight. He was as well read as anyone I'd ever met. He could run intellectual circles around any of my professors. He'd clearly thought about these issues with a depth and breadth few people can match. And yet he remained a committed, faithful Christian.

I found, and still find, enormous comfort in this. Our theologian guest speaker is not alone. Many of the brightest minds in the history of the world were and are committed Christians— still more believe in God. Philosophers, theologians, biologists, mathematicians—you'll find committed Christians at the top of their fields, across disciplines and across time. To think Christianity is intellectually bankrupt requires a special kind of ignorance about the history of human thought. Whatever questions you have, however difficult they may be, intelligent Christians—smarter than you or I—have wrestled with those questions and come out on the other side with their faith intact. That doesn't erase our questions or doubts. Belief can remain a struggle. But it's comforting, nonetheless. Even if *I* struggled to believe, even if *I* have my doubts, I never need to feel my beliefs aren't intellectually respectable. Even if faith comes with difficulty, faith isn't blind.

2

Why We Doubt Anyway

Doubt and the Sources of Nonbelief

"Seldom, very seldom, does complete truth belong to any human disclosure; seldom can it happen that something is not a little disguised or a little mistaken."

—JANE AUSTEN, *EMMA*

MY FRIEND BEN KNOWS Christian apologetics well. All those reasons to believe? Yeah, he's heard 'em. He's well-read in some of the strongest arguments for God's existence and the responses to objections. But the doubts remain. It's not that he finds the arguments for God too weak. But there's still the lingering, unrelenting questions. More evidence and clearer answers may not be the only solution but they sure would help. It'd all be so much easier if God would stop hiding, wouldn't it?

Since I know Ben well, I know he'll relish being compared to a medieval knight. Ben sometimes reminds me of the knight in the movie *The Seventh Seal*.[1] Set in the middle ages, the film tells the story of a knight returning home from the Crusades. He doubts his

1. Ingmar Bergman, dir., *The Seventh Seal* (1957).

faith and, on his journey home, encounters Death and challenges him to a game of chess. How's that for a plot? The knight's faith is as battered and beaten as his body. He struggles especially with God's hiddenness. Returning from war, he's surely seen his share of suffering and pain, but above all he wants to know: why isn't God more obvious? He rests during his journey in a small town and goes to the chapel to pray. He sees a cloaked figure he believes to be a priest and bares his soul. But the audience sees what he doesn't. The one to which he confesses is his foe, Death. The knight pleads,

> Is it so awfully unthinkable to conceive of God with one's senses? Why should he conceal himself in a fog of half-spoken promises and unseen miracles? How are we to believe the believers when we don't believe ourselves? What will become of us who want to believe but cannot? And what of those who neither will nor can believe?

Death nods at his complaint and the knight continues. "I want knowledge. Not belief. Not supposition. But knowledge. I want God to reach out to me, unveil his face, speak to me . . . I cry to him in the darkness, but sometimes it is as if there is no one there." Death replies simply, "Perhaps there is no one there."

The haunting scene frames the knight's doubt. He asks for what he knows he cannot get. He wants to know God doesn't exist, to see him with his own two eyes. It's a big ask. In *East of Eden*, John Steinbeck wrote, "The proofs that God does not exist are very strong, but in lots of people they are not as strong as the feeling that He does."[2] Steinbeck is right that many people *feel* God's existence more than they think it. But I wonder if the reverse is true for some people, too. We might find the arguments, the reasons to believe, strong, but we can't shake the persistent feeling of God's absence. We're unsatisfied with God's dealings with us. We know what healthy relationships look like, after all. I enjoy spending time with my wife: we go on walks, we travel, we watch *Seinfeld* reruns, we look at old pictures of our kids, or dream about the future. Our relationship flourishes in these special, tangible

2. Steinbeck, *East of Eden*, 69.

moments. But my relationship with God is different. And, if I'm honest, there are times when I wish it was more like my relationship with my wife: something tangible and clear. I have a relationship with God but, compared to my wife or friends, God sometimes seems hidden and remote.

We've now run into a different problem: the problem of divine hiddenness. It's like a sibling to the problem of evil. There are similarities, but they are different. Imagine a world without pain and suffering. Think Willy Wonka's chocolate factory but without the disappearing children. Everybody is happy, the Oompa-Loompas are dancing and singing, we're eating sweets to our heart's content, and we're floating around with antigravity candy. That's a world I can get behind. But even in our sugar-laden utopia without pain or suffering, God's silence would still trouble us. I may not feel the pangs of death or disease, but I'd be troubled by God's absence. We don't need to imagine a fairy-tale world to see how God's hiddenness is disturbing. Suppose your close friend has suddenly died from a rare blood disease. You're overwhelmed with grief. As you silently weep alone in your room, you hear God's whisper: "I know you're hurting. But I want you to know I love you, I'm with you, and everything's going to be okay." God's presence wouldn't remove your grief, but would it not offer some comfort? God's clear presence, however subtle, would be a great comfort to many of us. And so few of us experience it.

The problem of divine hiddenness is a major contributing factor in our doubt and nonbelief. When we experience God as hidden, we equate that with silence or absence—but the God we worship is neither. Why do we default to these patterns of thinking? Whether we recognize it or not, there are forces working behind the scenes priming us to think of God as hidden, absent, and silent. Through both nature and nurture, we're inclined to doubt. Because of this, even strong arguments and powerful personal experiences are not always enough for us. Like our medieval knight, we need more than faith. We crave knowledge. As with anything, understanding the problem is the first step to a solution. In this chapter, we'll explore the dynamics of doubt, nonbelief, and their sources. We'll start with a closer look at faith, nonbelief, and doubt. Then, we'll explore two sources of our doubt: sin and secularity.

It's All Greek to Me: The Difference in Faith and Belief

I like to argue. Growing up, friends and family often told me, "You should be a lawyer." It wasn't a compliment. Over my decades of arguing about everything from theology to sports to whether a knife or bat is a better weapon in a fight, I've noticed a lot of arguments are about how we use words. If it were up to me, all books would start with a glossary of key terms authors plan to use and how they'll use them. Okay, okay, I get it. We don't do that because glossaries are a snooze-fest. But it would help keep our words in order. I don't know about you, but I often find myself using words then wondering, "Wait, what does this even mean?" It's usually not a big deal—when we "peruse" a website, do we skim it or pay close attention to detail? The dictionary definition now makes both possible options. But sometimes our ambiguity is a big deal. Faith, doubt, and nonbelief are some of those tricky words we sometimes use without knowing what we mean by them.

If you've ever perused the New Testament, you probably noticed the words "believe" and "faith" show up a lot. They were favorites of Jesus. He often talked about the faith of others. He asked his disciples, for example, "Why are you afraid, you of little faith?" (Matthew 8:26). He also says things like, "Go—your faith has made you well!" (Mark 10:52). Jesus expects his followers to display faith. Jesus also encourages his hearers "to believe." He said things like, "Do not fear, only believe" (Mark 5:36) and "I am the resurrection and the life. Those who believe in me, even though they die, will live" (John 11:25). We're only skimming examples off the top. Faith and belief show up a lot. But their quantity doesn't make them important. A lot seems to be riding on *our* faith and belief. If we *believe* in Jesus, we'll live, even though we die? Sign me up. Following Jesus well means *believing* well, so how do we do it?

My high school chemistry teacher—who had the reputation of being something of a genius—liked to say, "I know every language but Greek." As high schoolers we were *just* gullible enough to fall into his trap. "Oh yeah," we'd asked armed with our extensive training in the French or Spanish alphabet. "What does '*les trois chiens*' mean?" He'd drop his punch line: "Sounds Greek to me." Hilarious. The New Testament really is Greek to us. Longtime attenders of church services have likely heard a preacher or two bust out the Greek in a sermon. You'll hear, "Well, in the Greek . . ." as half of the audience's eyes glaze over. If you listen carefully, though, you'll occasionally hear something enlightening. The Bible was written in different languages than our own, after all, and sometimes our translations are inadequate. There are nuances in the original languages which aren't always on the surface of our English translations. What it means to "believe" is one of those times.

Well, in the Greek—*snaps fingers* stay with me—the words for "believe" and "faith" are different versions of the same word. You can see the family resemblance yourself: in the New Testament, *pistis* is the Greek noun usually translated "faith" and *pisteuo* is the verb usually translated as "believe." You don't need a degree in the Greek language to see the similarity. But what do they mean? As is often the case, a word in another language has several options in English. Rarely do we find a one-to-one correspondence. In this case, the shared root of the words is something like "trust" or "allegiance." When Jesus commends someone for faith or encourages someone to believe, he's urging people to *trust* him. He wants his hearers to commit their lives to his ways and know he's worthy of our allegiance. Easy enough, right? What's the big deal?

Well, the rub is the English words we use in our translations don't always work like that. Faith usually does mean something like trust. Belief *can* work like that. When I say, "I believe in my wife," I mean something like "I trust my wife." To believe *in* something is to trust it and it requires our hearts as well as our heads. Easy enough. But we don't always use belief like that, do we? Do you believe Lee Harvey Oswald shot JFK? Do you believe Missouri is west of the Mississippi River? Do you believe Finland exists? We're displaying no trust when we say, "I believe in aliens." We're, instead, making a comment about what we *think*. When we talk about believing something, we often don't have trust in mind. What we have in mind is something in our minds: we believe *that* something is true or false. A good way to tell which way we're using "believe" is to notice the word which follows it: we believe *that* (something like "think") or believe *in* (something like trust). When Jesus encourages us to believe in him, he primarily has the latter in mind. He wants our trust, our allegiance. Of course, I'm not saying belief ("think") is never involved. But we've got to keep the emphasis in the right place. When Jesus asks us "to believe," he's asking us to trust.

Okay, this is starting to read like a glossary. Why does all this matter? I hope, first, it keeps us clear when we discuss faith and belief. When I talk about "belief," I mean something we do with our minds. Our Christian beliefs are when we think it's true that God exists, Jesus was God, or Jesus rose from the dead, to take a few examples. A "nonbeliever," then, is someone who *doesn't* believe the basic claims of Christianity. We've got believers in one camp and nonbelievers in another. Simple enough, right?

Well, no. You can probably tell I think it's rarely that simple. We might be clear on the difference between belief and nonbelief, but human beings usually resist simple categorization into "camps." It's probably more helpful to think of belief as a spectrum, with belief on one extreme and nonbelief on the other. While some people are on the extremes, many are somewhere in that mushy middle, too. We believe some things more strongly than others, do we not? I believe that I'm wearing shoes right now and Dover is the capital of Delaware, but I don't believe each with equal confidence. I *know* I'm wearing shoes. I'm not so sure about the capital of Delaware, though I *think* I'm right.[3] Some of our religious beliefs work like this, too. Some people are certain Jesus rose from the dead. Some are certain he didn't. And some think one or the other but aren't sure.

3. Update: a quick internet search confirmed Dover is the capital city of Delaware.

That's where doubt comes in. Doubt is when we lose confidence in something we believe. We can place doubt anywhere on that spectrum. Christian believers might have spare doubts occasionally but remain solidly committed to their beliefs. But sometimes doubt is more severe. When I talk about doubt, I'm usually thinking severe doubts. Severe doubts are those which can disrupt your faith. A Christian with severe doubts may still identify as a Christian and attend church, but the doubt is strong enough to cause her to reconsider whether it's all true or worth following. It's important to include doubts here because a lot of what I say will apply to those with doubts as much as to non-believers. But, hopefully, it's clear enough these are complicated categories and our individual experiences with doubt or belief can vary from person to person.

Worse than a glossary, this is starting to sound like a philosophy book. We don't want that. So let's pivot to the roots of doubt and nonbelief. While this book is about faith without belief, we'll do ourselves a disservice if we don't explore *why* we struggle with believing in God—either as individuals or a society. We could brainstorm a long list of sources of doubt or nonbelief, but two emerge as especially important: sin and secularity. Let's start with the more fundamental of the two, sin.

Hide and Seek: How Sin Clouds Our Vision

Why are villains usually the most memorable characters? Cartoon villains like Ursula, Cruella de Vil, and Jafar loom as large in my mind as their heroes. Long-running hero movie series like *James Bond* or *Batman* are distinguished in our minds by the delinquents that haunt them. Name a more iconic duo than Darth Maul and Darth Vader. Who can forget Heath Ledger's Joker? What about Hannibal Lecter, the Wicked Witch of the West, or the shark from *Jaws*? How many nightmares are made by Loki, Voldemort, or Gollum? One of my roommates in college had a spot-on Gollum voice. After I'd gone to bed, he enjoyed—like a scene from *The Tell-Tale Heart*—creeping to my room, slowly cracking the door, and craning his head slightly through the crack before letting out a skin-crawling "Smeaaagolllllll." I don't miss living with dudes.

Something about great villains sticks with us. We're almost drawn to them, but we're also repulsed by them. Gollum is a great example. Sniveling behind Sam and Frodo on their journey, he famously pursues the ring at all costs, calling it, "My precious." Because Gollum's mind is so warped by the ring, we feel, almost at the same time, both hatred toward and sympathy with Gollum. On the one hand, he's a ferocious, wicked, and selfish character. His mind is so warped by the ring he's willing to do anything—*anything*—to get it. But, on the other hand, that's why we feel sympathy: his mind is warped. He's almost schizophrenic, confusing who he is with the ring—or the part of him that can't do without it. The best villains do that to us. They repulse us. They are evil. We know they must be destroyed. But we can't help but feel pity for them. As Gandalf tells Frodo, it was pity which kept Bilbo from killing Gollum all those years ago.

I'm not one to try my hand at pop psychology, but I can't help but wonder if part of our pity and repulsion toward villains is because we see glimmers of ourselves in them. I recently read Gustave Flaubert's *Madame Bovary*. It's almost two hundred years old so I don't feel obliged to give a spoiler alert, but, you should read it, so I won't give too much away. Flaubert's Emma Bovary isn't the scorched-earth villain we're used to seeing in hero stories. She's a housewife who dreams of bigger and better things—and better men than her husband. Emma becomes entangled in affairs despite the faithful (even if boring) love of her Charles. But what's so haunting about Emma is her self-destructive patterns of thought that we can easily see in ourselves. Flaubert says of her, "Her will, like the veil her hat caught back with a cord, flutters in every breeze; always there is some desire urging her on, some convention restraining her."[4] Her desire overcomes convention. Entangled in a web of lies and debt, Emma becomes increasingly self-deceptive—and outright deceptive toward others. She's mostly selfish and inconsiderate. She allows a false, idealized picture

4. Flaubert, *Madame Bovary*, 78.

of reality to crowd out gratitude for her otherwise good life. And, most frightening of all, she often reminds me of myself.

A famous (and possibly apocryphal) story makes the point well. When *The Times of London* posed an important question to many prominent authors: "What's wrong with the world today?," one reply stole the show:

> Dear Sir,
>
> I am.
>
> Yours,
>
> G. K. Chesterton[5]

There is, in fact, much wisdom in Chesterton's response. We're quick to lay blame on others without giving much thought to our own depravity. A famous quote about a plank in your eye comes to mind. The old theological word for our depravity is "sin." Sin is a religious word we avoid when we can. It sounds harsh. It evokes street preachers with megaphones pointing out individuals and loudly labeling them, "SINNER!" We'd much prefer therapeutic categories, suggesting instead our wrong actions are the result of a faulty psyche. Something in our childhood or some chemical imbalance must be to blame. How else could someone go so wrong? No doubt, trauma or a chemical imbalance *can* poison our minds. But we can't avoid sin. Sin is the ultimate cause and effect of the fall—and the fall we've each experienced. God's good, ordered creation becomes disordered when humans *sin*— or disobey God—and we are infected with *sin* thereafter. So sin refers both to the symptoms (our wrong actions) and the disease itself (our broken nature). In both senses, our sin disrupts God's plans for us. When we sin, we choose a different vision for our life than the one he offers.

The early chapters of Genesis tell the story of God's good creation and our fall into sin. When God created humans, he

---

5. On his blog, historian Jordan M. Poss says the quote was originally, "The answer to the question, 'What is Wrong?' is, or should be, 'I am wrong.'" For more on the origins of the quote see: https://www.jordanmposs.com/blog/2019/2/27/whats-wrong-chesterton.

made us in his image. We're like a beautiful statue God carved to reflect his beauty to the rest of the world. But when we sin, it's as if we took a bucket of muck and mire and dumped it on our own heads. The statue is there, but its beauty is obscured by the mud. The initial act of mud-dumping was when Adam and Eve did the one thing God asked them not to do: They ate from the tree. Deceived by the serpent, they disobeyed God. Like the serpent promised, their "eyes were opened." But they couldn't see as they'd hoped. Instead of wisdom, they felt naked and ashamed. Instead of knowledge of good, they knew evil. Their eyes were opened, but not to God. We read,

> They heard the sound of the LORD God walking in the garden at the time of the evening breeze, and the man and his wife hid themselves from the presence of the LORD God among the trees of the garden. But the LORD God called to the man, and said to him, "Where are you?" He said, "I heard the sound of you in the garden, and I was afraid, because I was naked; and I hid myself." (Genesis 3:8–9)

Adam and Eve, who were made by God and for God, are *now afraid of God*. Things are no longer "very good." Things are no longer how God made them to be. Their relationship with God and with each other is broken.

Genesis 3 is illuminating but we shouldn't read it as merely a history lesson. It teaches us a lot about who *we* are and what it means to live in a fallen world—if we'll listen. We see, for example, what sin encourages us to do. Our sin encourages us to hide from God. We're ashamed, maybe even angry, at God when we wrong him. So we hide in the bushes. We talk of the "problem of divine hiddenness," but the first problem of hiddenness is the other way around: not God hiding from humans, but humans hiding from God. Sin will do that. Our sin obstructs our vision of God. We don't like to think of ourselves as to blame, of course. Like Madame Bovary, we're duplicitous and deceiving, doing what it takes to get our way without giving two hoots what it does to the people around us. Our obsession with ourselves and our own advancement erodes

God's image in us. But, most troubling, we hide from God. Theologians call this the "noetic effect of sin": Our minds are dulled and no longer see God as we were designed to see him. We ask why God is hidden, but we should notice how we don't have eyes to see because of our sin. "Our eyes are opened" to the ugly and broken things of the world, but not to God.

I once heard a Christian professor tell stories about his seminary students struggling with doubt. After many years of this, he noticed a pattern. So, one day, when a young man came into his office and started confessing doubts about Christianity, the professor bluntly asked, "When did you start sleeping with your girlfriend?" The pattern the professor noticed was some sort of sin (and, because he's dealing with college students, usually sexual sin) preceded their doubts. He noticed sin is the root of doubt. Of course, it doesn't mean some specific sin is always behind any of our doubts. But the professor was onto something important: We're not attentive enough to the connection between what we think and how we act. We think of ourselves as better than that, as if our beliefs are simply a virtuous submission to the evidence. But our heads and hearts are more intertwined than many of us care to admit. If you cheat on your partner, give it time and you'll justify it with "reasons." You'll find "flaws" you didn't see before. In a similar way, when our hearts and desires direct us away from God, we'll find it's easier to doubt him. We'll find our reasons, even if none existed before.

It may seem like I'm implying all we need to do is get our act together and we'll see God everywhere. I'm not. But when God isn't another "thing" in the universe, another thing for us to see or touch, our sinful eyes must be trained to see God's activity in the world. On this side of heaven, we'll never see God as we were created to see him. Our sinful thoughts and actions play an important role in clouding our vision of God. But our recognition of the effects of sin already attunes us to think of God's "hiddenness" differently. Blaming God for his hiddenness only makes the problem worse. We must own our role in God's hiddenness before we can have eyes to see him well.

Blind Leading the Blind: The Sources of Doubt in Our Culture

Have you heard the one about the fish in water? Two fish are swimming along, enjoying the current, when they pass another fish on his way to work. The fish nods and says, "How's the water today, fellas?" The two fish nod back and keep swimming along. A few minutes later, one fish looks at his buddy and says, "What the heck is water?"

It's a bad joke, I know. But it almost perfectly illustrates a simple point: There are some things so basic or fundamental to us we don't even recognize we think this way. Whether or not others think this way is beside the point. We all have our water we swim in. We may not even know there are land animals. A good example of this for many Americans is democracy. We tend to think of the democratic ideal as an obvious good. Suppose a friend said, "I think we should abolish the republic and crown a king instead, whose line of succession is determined by the firstborn male." In the United States, such a claim is more likely to be interpreted as a sarcastic joke—*obviously* too stupid to be taken seriously—rather than a real suggestion. The reason we instinctively think this way is not because we've weighed the pros and cons of democracy against alternatives. We instinctively think this way because of the water we swim in. Many countries, in fact, *do* have monarchies. We may know this, of course, but it's unlikely that we've considered monarchy as a live option for our country. I'm not calling us to abandon democracy in favor of monarchy. The basic point is that we take so many things for granted depending on the group or society of which we're a part. It's the water in which we swim.

In our Western society today, there are a lot of ways to describe the water we swim in. We might call ourselves "technological," on account of our obsession with screens and digital devices. We might call ourselves "capitalistic," to reflect our obsession with money. You might've also heard academic jargon like "postmodern" applied to our world. We're all these things and more. But surely we're also an age of doubt. When reconfiguring how

33

to think about Christianity over fifty years ago, Alistair Kee said, "Ours is an age of faith, but not belief."[6] As he saw it, belief in God was on the way out, so Christianity needed to reconfigure itself and drop the emphasis on belief. Echoing Kee's sentiment about the state of our age, philosopher Charles Taylor more recently (and more influentially) said ours was a "secular age."[7] Taylor's project is historical. He's tracing the history of religious belief or belief in the supernatural over several hundred years. When he calls our age "secular," he doesn't mean we've abandoned God or religion—though, that clearly describes our culture in some ways, too. By a secular age, Taylor means we've come to see belief in God as one option among others.[8] To put it another way, it wouldn't shock us to meet an atheist or agnostic. More pointedly and personally, we see atheism or agnosticism as live options in our culture. Even if you can't *personally* imagine it because of your faith or family relationships, a rejection of faith and God is a real alternative for people in our society. We tend to see all beliefs, even religious ones, like a buffet: you can take a little of this, a little of that, or whatever suits you. God just isn't everyone's cup of tea, so some people opt for something else.

You might be thinking, "Yeah, and what's strange about that?" And that's the point. Because that's the water we swim in, we hardly consider alternatives. Not every age, however, was inflicted with doubt like our own. One of the great ironies about Bergman's "medieval" knight struggling with God's absence is he sounds so modern. That's not to say medieval people didn't struggle with God's hiddenness. But the thirst for knowledge, as opposed to faith, is a distinctly modern one. Our tendency, too, to see God as "hidden" from the world is a modern one. We think like the knight. We're *trained* to think that way.

6. Kee, *Way of Transcendence*, ix.

7. Though released almost twenty years ago, Taylor's work has inspired a lot of discussion, especially in the last several years. If you want to tackle the tome, see Taylor, *A Secular Age*.

8. Smith, *How (Not) to Be Secular*, 21. If you want the meat of Taylor without the many side dishes (like his *excursus* on carnival), Smith's introduction is super helpful.

One of the ways we're trained to think that way is to think through a scientific paradigm. But we're better off calling this "scientism" rather than "science." Science is a wonderful thing. Science illuminates our physical world. It teaches us how our body, environment, and universe behave. But *scientism* is the tendency to see the scientific as the best or even the *only* way to know. You can see this with the knight: only knowledge can satisfy, and knowledge is what we can sense. We only *know* what we feel, taste, smell, see, or hear. In public discourse, ideological opponents will insist they are "following the science," as if it's the highest standard of truth we can achieve. To be perceived as "anti-science" is the death knell to any view. We rightly see science as useful, but we slip into *scientism* when we make it ultimate. We slip into scientism when we, like Carl Sagan, think "the cosmos is all there is" because science tells me so. Scientism is a pattern of thinking that dominates our age.

It wasn't always so. Many non-Western cultures today, or Western cultures prior to the so-called "Enlightenment," were infused with the supernatural in a way unimaginable to many of us today. It's even more difficult to imagine in a place like the United States, where our collective memory only stretches back a few hundred years. The scent of the supernatural, even if it's been resoundingly rejected, lingers on in older countries. My wife and I lived in Scotland for a bit. While visiting the Isle of Skye with my sister and brother-in-law, we visited a place called "Fairy Glen." When we arrived in this magical, green alcove, my sister asked, "Where are the boats?" She thought it was called "Ferry Glen," apparently, and expected to see large ships transporting cars. Alas, we didn't see any fairies, either. But fairies still feature prominently in Scottish folklore. Certain wooded areas or waterways were thought to be the haunts of magical creatures, to whom visitors should give deference.

I don't know the extent to which the locals, even hundreds of years ago, really believed *all* the stories about their local fairies. But it's clear our ancestors' imaginations were shaped by the supernatural in a way ours is not. Apart from the characters of their histories and folklore, they were quicker to attribute supernatural causes to otherwise natural events than we are today. They saw the world as governed not merely by impersonal natural laws, but by personal, spiritual forces. Be they demons, angels, or, yes, fairies, to live in our world was to be aware and sensitive to another. This isn't merely an ancient phenomenon. Many cultures today, especially in the Global South, can relate. Their world is not contained to the physical and material. Our world isn't a machine. It's wider, deeper, and infused with the supernatural. But we're trained to wave such cultures away as "backward" or, the ultimate insult, "medieval," who languish in darkness without modern science.

It's not difficult to see why, in a secular age, belief in God is sometimes difficult. For our ancestors, it came naturally. For us, doubt usually wins the day. If our culture had a patron saint, Thomas is a good candidate. Thomas has received the unfortunate nickname "Doubting Thomas" because of his need for evidence. When told Jesus had, indeed, rose from the dead, Thomas was skeptical. I mean, can you blame him? He'd just been told a dead man—a man he *knew* to be dead—got up out of his grave. To tag him with the moniker "Doubting" because of that seems a bit harsh. But Thomas needed proof. Not unlike our medieval knight, he wanted to know. He said, "Unless I see the mark of the nails in his hands, and put my finger in the mark of the nails and my hand in his side, I will not believe" (John 20:25). Later, Jesus appeared to the disciples and Thomas was present. Jesus gave Thomas the opportunity of a lifetime: to feel the wounds Jesus was given on the cross. His doubt dissolves into belief as he confesses, "My Lord and my God!" (John 20:28). He's a good candidate for our patron saint because we relate to Thomas. Our secular age plays the Doubting Thomas role. We want knowledge and evidence. We want what we can see, hear, or touch.

What explains our age's doubt and unbelief? Questions like this never have only one answer. It's a complicated potion of ingredients we've taken. But our cultural imagination tells us a story about the triumph of science. As we learn more and more about the physical laws that govern the universe—this story goes—so we have less and less need for supernatural explanations. Sure, our ancestors believed in demons and sometimes used them to explain earthquakes and mental illness, but now we know the mechanics of plate tectonics and psychology. Of course, there's probably a grain of truth here. We're more likely to reach for supernatural explanations when we can't find a physical one. But this story won't do. It's not as if our ancestors were ignorant of nature. Thomas didn't need to be taught the science of decomposition to know dead people stay dead. Our knowledge of *physical* explanations is sometimes more comprehensive than what our ancestors had access to, but the difference is quantitative not qualitative. They knew, after all, there was a physical world with its own kind of movements and logic. But they saw (clearer than we) that our categories of "natural" and "supernatural" are not necessarily at odds. They were able to see layers of meaning when we're often too myopic. The waters we swim in are secular waters.

Some aspects of our secularity are unavoidable. But Christians should resist, specifically, the bifurcation between nature and supernature. For Christians, the key which unlocks all doors is the incarnation: our theology, philosophy, ethics, and living begins and ends with Jesus Christ. The church teaches Jesus is one person in two natures: human and divine. Early church teaching, though, couldn't leave it at that. They insisted, thanks to the testimony of Scripture, that Jesus was no mixture of a god and a human. It's not as if we add a god-mind, some human limbs, mixed it all together and got Jesus, the half-man, half-god. Church teaching roundly rejects this. Instead, we say Jesus is *fully* man and *fully* God. He is *truly* man and *truly* God. In our secular age, we find this incredible—maybe even impossible—because we think of humanity and divinity as incompatible. But the church has always confessed Jesus is fully *both*. He didn't need to sacrifice some of his divinity to become a man or to sacrifice some of his humanity to remain God. This tells us something important about our world: our physical, natural world can be infused with divinity without giving up what it is. There's no tug-of-war.

What's this mean for a secular age? It means, at least, we should reorient our thinking about what is "natural" and "supernatural." That's difficult to do because, again, it's the water we swim in. Trying to think otherwise is like asking a fish to breathe out of water. But, hey, frogs exist, right? We may never fully shake our instinctive division between natural and supernatural. It certainly won't happen overnight. But a Christian view of the world must try to shake it. A Christian view of the world is infused with God's grace. God is present everywhere. Jesus Christ is the prime example but it's true elsewhere: God makes himself present to us *through* creation, not against it. We do see, hear, and touch God, but we do it mediated through his good and beautiful creation. If we're trained to see the world as merely natural, we'll be trained to see God nowhere.

It's no use pining for a pre-modern world where belief comes easy again. We *are* a secular age and we must, to some extent, play the hand we're dealt. While it's worth being critical of the domination of scientism and secularity, we can recognize how science and other ways of knowing do bring many goods. But we must be aware of how we're trained to see the world. Fighting against nurture can be an uphill battle. Many of us are a Doubting Thomas and don't see another way out. Hopefully, recognizing we live in a secular age helps us see that it doesn't have to be this way. We've erected obstacles to belief. But the obstacles aren't insurmountable.

Where Does This Leave Us?

Sin and secularity are two sources of our doubt and nonbelief. I'm convinced a deeper understanding of each will help anyone struggling to believe in the claims of Christianity. But even if they can help explain our doubt, they're no antidote. Doubt and nonbelief are still with us. Ben, for one, really feels it. He knows we live in a secular age and knows the Christian story includes sin. He has the humility to admit his judgment can be clouded. Still, the doubt lingers on. He feels stuck in it. He wants to decide. He wants to commit. He knows the decision is so, so, so important. But he fears making the wrong choice.

Yet, ever the philosophical thinker, Ben finds himself drawn to a philosophical school of thought called "pragmatism." The pragmatists are, well, pragmatic. They focus on what works, on what's useful. When it comes to belief, we should act on what makes sense. Though many of our beliefs happen to us—I can't stop believing that I'm looking at a computer as I type this—some of them are more complicated. In a landmark essay, philosopher William James argued we can "will to believe."[9] I live not far from a hiker's paradise called Red River Gorge—known to climbers as the "red" and to the rest of us as the "gorge." Every year, motivated hikers set out and get lost on a trail. Sometimes they get themselves so lost out there they don't make it or have to be helicoptered out. I've never gotten lost (I'm not exactly a risk-taker) but I know friends who have. They recount a moment when you must decide: are we walking this way or that way? Are we making camp for the night or fighting the darkness? And there's no such thing as not deciding. Not to decide is to decide. And they aren't sure about their decisions, but they press on anyway. They must press on anyway.

Sometimes, James argues, belief is like being lost on a hike. In fact, religious belief is perhaps the best example. We come to a crossroads and the paths are laid out before us. Not to decide is to decide—the agnostic bets her chips like the rest of us. Ben feels the pull of a choice. He recognizes not to decide is to decide. Sometimes, the only option available to us is to press on with a path, even when we're uncertain where it'll lead. This doesn't mean our choice is random. The lost hiker picks the path which seems best based on something—for example, maybe the path they *think* leads back to base camp. There's uncertainty, to be sure. But it's not a blind guess. For religious belief, there's one path worth exploring more: faith without belief.

---

9. James, *Writings 1878–1899*, 445.

3

Help Thou My Unbelief

Faith without Belief

"Hope—which, below, spurs love of the true good."

—DANTE, *PARADISO*

IN ONE OF MY most vivid memories from my childhood, I sat in the backseat of our van, staring out the window as the sun receded over a freshly harvested cornfield, and wondering who I was going to marry. I couldn't have been older than twelve or thirteen. My parents were in the front and my sister was probably sitting next to me, but I don't remember for sure. What I do remember is driving home from Owensboro, a town about thirty minutes north of where I grew up. I grew up in Beaver Dam, Kentucky. As the name implies, there's not much to do in Beaver Dam. So we went to Owensboro to have fun (people from Owensboro laugh when I say that). My family probably drove to Owensboro a hundred times when I was growing up. Looking out the window and dreaming about my future spouse was one of the only times I remember. Maybe I was feeling especially contemplative. Maybe there was something odd in the rice I ate for dinner. I don't know what it was, but I felt overwhelmed thinking about my future. Who would I marry? How many kids would I have? An odd feeling fell over me when I absorbed the fact I wouldn't be twelve (or thirteen) forever. I tried to imagine what it'd be like to be an adult. I couldn't. I *knew* I would get married. Almost every adult I knew was married, after all. That was the way of the world in Beaver Dam. But I couldn't imagine *her*. I naively assumed she'd be someone I knew at the time. Perhaps a classmate or friend from church. But, for whatever reason, I remember gratitude washing over me when I reflected on one fact: I didn't live in a country where arranged marriages were the norm.

When you grow up in the Bible Belt, you read a lot of the Bible. For those readers of the Bible out there, you know the Bible can be a foreign place. Most of us struggle to understand the cultural world of the middle east today. How can we expect to understand it two thousand, or four thousand, years ago? It seems odd to us. People ride on donkeys and camels. They don't watch TV. But, in my young mind, near the top of the list of biblical oddities was arranged marriages. How could anyone expect to love someone they didn't choose for themselves? Through high school (and into college), my parents would occasionally drop not-so-subtle hints about girls I should consider dating. Almost certainly because it was *their* suggestion and not *mine*, I always hated the idea. "What if *they* got to choose my wife?," I'd sometimes think, always relieved they didn't.

As I have matured, the idea of arranged marriages is still, of course, foreign to me. I *am* married now (no, I didn't know her when I was twelve). We chose each other and I'm so glad we did. But, on this side of the dating scene, I've come to see some wisdom in arranged marriage. That's not to say I think it's a good idea. I doubt my son or daughter will, either. But there's a reason why this ancient practice lives on, even in parts of the world today. In an article with an absurd title—"Why You Should Treat Marriage More Like a Business"—from a few years ago, NBC News cited a study that placed the divorce rate of arranged marriages at *four percent.*[1] At the time, the divorce rate for marriages in which spouses picked their partner was around 40 percent. If the results of those polls held, it means you'd be around 900 percent more likely to get a divorce if you picked your spouse than if someone else picked for you. I know, I know. In countries with arranged marriages, there are other cultural differences at play besides arranged marriages, which could suppress the divorce rate. But this should still confound many of our expectations that unless we choose who we marry, we'll surely be unhappy and seek divorce. This, evidentially, is not the case.

We don't need to draw too many conclusions from this, but one is worth drawing: Commitment to a spouse is not necessarily tied to our feelings before our vows. For many of us, this is completely counterintuitive. I'll probably sound old when I say this, but the contemporary dating scene seems like such a mess from the outside. I'm not sure how many daters out there are looking for marriage. But for those that are, for those who see dating as a gateway to marriage, the goal of dating is discernment. You want to see if this person is right for such a big commitment. Dating is almost like buying a house. Whether you write it out or not, you have a list of "must haves" and "wants." You know you won't get everything on your list, but you hope you get enough to be happy with it. You're looking for compatibility, chemistry, and, above all, love. So the dating discernment process can be long and intense.

Given the divorce rates, and that people understandably want to avoid the way of divorced friends, parents, or relatives, it makes sense to erect safeguards. It's a good idea, after all, to see whether this person is a good fit. And yet there's something missing in this approach. Without getting *too* romantically sacramental, I'll only say the marriage vows on the altar of the church should be the greatest safeguard of divorce. Your feelings are no safeguard. Your feelings will change. What matters is *commitment.* The common saying "the honeymoon is over" says it all: The heart-eyed infatuation you feel during dating, engagement, your wedding day, and

1. https://www.nbcnews.com/better/pop-culture/why-you-should-treat-marriage-more-business-ncna778551.

that beautiful week in Maui will fade. What's left are the promises you make on the altar to remain faithful and love despite your feelings. I don't mean to be dour. My wife and I love each other and *feel* deep love for each other. Thanks to the commitments at the altar, that love grows deeper, stronger—but it is different than when we dated. Our commitment, not our feelings, built our marriage. It's a message arranged marriages can't avoid.

As I've reflected on arranged marriages, and that time in the car on the way home from Owensboro, I've sometimes wondered if any of this wisdom can be extended to faith. Faith in Jesus *isn't* an arranged marriage. Like all analogies, it breaks down. But there are important parallels. In this chapter, we'll explore how commitment and fidelity to someone can take precedence over how we feel—or even what we *think*.

Help Thou My Unbelief

Jesus once encountered a frantic father. I can relate. When my son was a baby, he caught a nasty fever. It shot up to nearly 105, which is an unsafe level. It is the marker when most pediatricians say you should take him to the ER. More frightening still, his breathing was labored and uncomfortable. The most emotionally exhausting moments of my life were taking care of my sick baby boy because I felt helpless. Since his breathing was labored, we took him to the ER for the first time. Thankfully, everything was fine. But it's a terrible feeling when something is wrong with your son. You want to find a solution and fast. You'll do anything. I don't know what I'd do if I thought my son had an "unclean spirit." In Mark 9, we read about a father whose son has an unclean spirit. The text doesn't say exactly how long it had afflicted his son, but it suggests it's been going on for years. It's hard not to read exasperation in the father's voice. So imagine what must go through his mind when he hears about the roving band of Jews who have the power to *heal*.

The father finds Jesus's disciples first. But they can't deliver on his hopes. His son remains afflicted with the unclean spirit. The crowd—apparently, a crowd has formed at this point?—is arguing about something. That's what crowds do best. Then, they see Jesus. They all rush to him and the father fills Jesus in. He tells him how this unclean spirit is afflicting his son. He impresses the gravity of the situation: The demonic spirit in his son tries to kill him. It tosses him into fire or water. And the ER can't treat demons. Because the father has tried everything, he must be wondering whether anything can help. So he says to Jesus, "If you are able to do anything, have pity on us and help us" (Mark 9:22). You can sense the desperation. He doesn't know if this will help, but, at this point, he's willing to try anything. He doesn't know if Jesus can help. But why not try?

Jesus responds, "'If you are able!'—All things can be done for the one who believes." The father responds, "I believe! Help my unbelief."

When reading the passage, it's easy to glaze over the father's response. But let's look closer. Is the father's response a confession of faith? Doubt? Or both? In the same breath, he says he believes but also that he's stuck in unbelief. What's going on?

In his *Sermons on the New Testament Lessons*, Saint Augustine notices the tension. He says the father's "I believe" shows he has faith but the "Help my unbelief" shows there was not *full* faith.[2] Augustine is surely onto something. He points to the apostles as an example. While they are exemplars of great faith on the one hand, they also ask for an increase of faith on the other (Luke 17:5). We see, too, examples of the weakness of their faith. With Augustine, all believers should see the father *in themselves*. We may have faith, and yet our faith is incomplete and imperfect. It is being perfected by Jesus Christ through the power of the Holy Spirit, but we're not there yet. Augustine is right, then: We need God's help in our unbelief. So we should relate to the father in this way.

And yet I think there's more going on in this passage. The dichotomy is too stark. Nowhere else in the New Testament are "belief" and "unbelief" set side by side and connected in this way. It leads me to wonder how the father can, simultaneously, be an

---

2. Augustine, *Sermons on the New Testament Lessons*, Sermon 30. https://www.newadvent.org/fathers/160330.htm.

example of belief and unbelief. We've already encountered the difficulties in translating the Greek word. The father's confession uses the same root: I believe, and yet I need help with my unbelief. How can we make sense of this?

It goes without saying that we can't get into the mind of the father. We can't know what's happening in his mind or heart. We can only guess. But there are some clues in the passage that may help. We see the dynamic between belief and unbelief from the beginning of the passage. On the one hand, the father is open to Jesus's healing touch. On the other, he's not yet convinced. He says to Jesus, "*if* you can do anything." His doubt does not go unnoticed. In a not-so-subtle rebuke, Jesus repeats the man's words to him, "if you can" in a way that suggests the punctuation "!?!?!?" It's as if to say, "are you out of your mind??? Of course I can!!!" After Jesus tells him he must believe, the man confesses: "I believe! Help my unbelief." Jesus often explicitly condones or condemns the level of faith in his encounters. But, in this passage, he's notably silent on the matter. That Jesus then heals the boy suggests that the man displays the kind of faith Jesus is looking for, but the text stops short from saying as much. Jesus does not, as he does elsewhere, commend the father's faith, but the boy's unclean spirit is eradicated nonetheless. It appears the father does express faith or trust in Jesus, but simultaneously recognizes his unbelief as a problem he needs help with.

A key that helps unlock the father's dual confession is the father's very confession of unbelief and cry for help. We should notice his cry for help is *itself* an expression of his faith. When he cries in desperation, "help me with my unbelief" *he expresses his faith*. In this light, it's easy to see how the second sentence follows naturally from the first. The father *trusts* Jesus, but he can't yet *believe*. So he does the only thing he can do: he asks Jesus for help. A natural interpretation of the passage, then, is that the father expresses faith—trust or allegiance—but struggles to believe in his mind. We could say his cry "help my unbelief!" is the father's hoping his mind catches up to his heart. This dynamic is present elsewhere in the passage, too. He feels the pull to Jesus and rushes to him for help. But, despite this, he can't quite bring himself to *believe* Jesus can heal his son. *"If you are able to do anything,"* he says to Jesus. Can you blame him? The guy has tried it all. He's seen remedy after remedy fail. If you asked him, *"Can* Jesus heal your son?" I'm not sure he could've confidently answered in the affirmative. He's a doubter. A nonbeliever. He's not convinced. Yet, he musters the trust and faith necessary to bring his son before Jesus and ask for help. The man has faith *despite* his unbelief.

Faith Seeking Belief

One of the long-standing debates in Christian theology is an answer to the question, "Where do we start?" The medieval theologian Saint Anselm wrote one of the most famous sentences in the history of Christian theology when he started with "faith seeking understanding." Mulling the proper approach to philosophy or theology, Anselm proposed we begin with faith and, with that as our starting point, move from there toward understanding. He proposed, in other words, starting with faith rather than skepticism. We don't start by understanding God so we can trust him. We trust God so that we might understand him. Anselm exemplified this posture of "faith seeking understanding" in his writings. His brilliant works of philosophy and theology were often penned as *prayers*. He begins one with, "Come then, Lord my God, teach my heart where and how to seek you, where and how to find you."

Unfortunately, Anselm's dictum "faith seeking understanding" sounds foreign to modern ears. It's not the way we're taught to think in a secular age. We're schooled in what we can call "Enlightenment thinking," or thinking in the manner of that historical movement in the last five hundred years we call the "Enlightenment." A hallmark of Enlightenment thinking is beginning with skepticism, even extreme skepticism. Like a reflex hammer to a knee, our minds pop with skepticism. Following our medieval knight, we thirst for *knowledge*, not faith. Perhaps the clearest picture of our reflexive skepticism is the philosopher Descartes. Famously, Descartes ran an experiment to test whether he existed.

He wondered: What if my experience of reality is only a dream or a scenario manipulated by an evil demon? How can I prove it's *not* that? Descartes's escape route was his now famous claim, "I think, therefore I am."[3] Because he can ask the question in the first place, he reasoned, he can find stable ground on which to think. Setting his answer aside, what's extraordinary is Descartes felt the need to ask the question in the first place. Do I exist? Sheesh. And I thought *I* was skeptical. But that is Enlightenment thinking. Descartes and his progeny are our teachers. We're inheritors of Enlightenment thinking. We begin with as few assumptions as possible and reason from an unbiased perspective. And that's why many of us flip Anselm on his head: Our approach is understanding seeking faith. We must start on solid, well-reasoned ground, then proceed to faith. That's a hallmark of our secular age.

But it doesn't have to be this way. We don't have to dismiss Anselm as a medieval bumpkin. Maybe, just maybe, he was onto something. We *can* start with faith. But we've got an enormous problem. We've got an imagination problem. Because of sin and secularity, many of us have the hardest time imagining what faith without belief looks like. Our tendency is to start with a solid belief that something exists and only then can we trust it. There's an important and right insight in there, after all. There's a reason I started the book with reasons for God. But what happens when the arguments aren't persuasive? A secular age or Enlightenment thinking tells you, "Give it up. If *you're* not convinced, it's not worth your time." But I don't think that's right and I'm not alone. It's true that it won't be easy. Faith without belief requires a reorientation of our default patterns of thought. So we need *something* to help us imagine what faith seeking understanding is like. For that, let's return to arranged marriages.

Arranged marriages seem so foreign to us because they flip modern assumptions about dating, love, and marriage on their heads. One of those assumptions about marriage is we start with love. We feel love first, this I know, because the rom-com tells me so. In any rom-com worth its salt, there's always *that moment*. You

---

3. But let's see Descartes escape *The Truman Show.*

know the moment. The guy and gal *just know*. Or, when it's not love at first sight, the moment still strikes them at some point. Dropping their previous pride and prejudice, our Darcy and Lizzy finally see one another with fresh eyes of infatuation. They know they're made for each other. And that, we're told, is what love is. It's the magical, tingly feeling you get inside. If you don't feel it then by golly you're not in love. You *feel* first. Then you date. Sure, maybe there are bumps along the way. But as long as we feel our love strongly enough, our love can carry us to the altar—and beyond!

Our popular imagination is shaped by this story. The story is reinforced by our cultural altar. In a recent rewatch of the NBC comedy series *Parks and Recreation*, I was struck by the wedding scenes. They are all so *cute*. April and Andy marry in their living room while the groom is wearing a Colts jersey. Ron and Diane marry on a whim, upstairs at a judge's office. Ben and Leslie, like Ron and Diane, make a last-minute decision to wed, but they marry in the Parks and Rec office. The show captures the essence of each couple so well. That's why they're cute. But, in my recent rewatch, something struck me that never had previously. Something was missing. Something wasn't right. There was a gap in the center of these wedding scenes. Then it hit me. There are no vows! There are no promises. The "vows" are replaced by recitations of each individual's feelings toward the other one. In other words, they tell each other what they like about the other. It makes for good television. But does it make for a good marriage?

In a culture like ours, arranged marriages are virtually impossible. Why? Because arranged marriages *cannot* share our culture's assumptions about marriage. There can be no fuzzy feelings. Each spouse *can't* say what they like about the other. They don't know each other! *The moment* when the couple knows is, and must be, at the altar, while promising their lives to one other. The rom-com knows no way of fitting an arranged marriage into its story. Now, this is no apologetic for arranged marriages. Neither is it a call to rush into marriage. I can imagine the flood of angry emails now. But, if we let our cultural assumptions rest for a moment, there are a couple of things I think we can learn from arranged marriages.

First, arranged marriages show us how commitment takes precedence in an important, lifelong decision. When we assume the rom-coms are right, we must *know* we're compatible with a prospective spouse. We must *know* we like this person *a lot*. We must *know* this person's favorite flavor of ice cream and putt-putt skill level. It's hard to imagine entering a marriage without these things. But marriages can succeed without them. The way they succeed is placing the commitment front and center. The vows and promises we make at the altar secure lifelong fidelity, even when our spouse fails us or changes. And here's an important secret about people: People change. You change. Your spouse will change. The person you marry will not be the same person you celebrate your tenth anniversary with, who will not be the same person you celebrate your twenty-fifth anniversary with. Because we all change. How can a marriage last without commitment? Promises outlast fuzzy feelings.

A second thing we learn from arranged marriages is self-denial. We tend to orient important life decisions around ourselves. What will make *me* happy? What will allow me to succeed or hit my goals? One of the (admittedly many) reasons arranged marriages are culturally counterintuitive, I think, is that they mean marriage *is not about me and my happiness*. What a radical idea! In the movies, divorces or separations are often justified by an appeal to happiness: "I just wasn't happy anymore," we're told. And we sympathize. It's no surprise. The "marriage is about my happiness" philosophy is the quickest path to high divorce rates. Instead, marriage should be about self-giving love. Jesus, as he so often did, said it best: When you look for yourself, you'll lose yourself; when you give up yourself, that's when you find yourself. Marriages reflect the larger Christian life because they—paradoxically—only work when they are self-giving. It's a difficult reorientation, one that takes most of us a lifetime of being shaped by the Holy Spirit. But the idea of faith is we give ourselves to Jesus in the hopes—in the knowledge—that he'll give himself to us in return. He's the only hope for a truly satisfying and fulfilling life.

I get it. Arranged marriage is a rather extreme way to make these points. Sometimes the extremes help drive home the principle but let's turn to another good example of marital commitment. In a rare vision of virtue from Hollywood, NBC's *The Office* provides a beautiful contrast to the sterile "vows" in *Parks and Rec*. In the final episode of the final season, Dwight Schrute and Angela Martin are finally wed. Though cute in its own way, Dwight and Angela's wedding has something the *Parks and Rec* weddings do not: a vision of lifelong commitment detached from how they feel in this moment. Following Schrute tradition, Dwight and Angela are standing in their burial plots. That is, their future graves. For, as the minister reminds them, it is the "only escape from what they are about to do."

Whether the show intended to make this point or not, Dwight and Angela's wedding recognizes the instability of fleeting feelings as a basis for marriage. They do not doubt their love for one another in that moment. But they, wisely, recognize the moment will pass. The "honeymoon phase" will be over soon. Their feelings will fade. And they must get on with the difficult, but fulfilling, task of loving each other "as long as they both shall live." A marriage based on feelings is a marriage based on uncertainty and instability. Ironically, it's only when we recognize the instability of our own feelings—we doubt our future selves, if you will—that we recognize our need for commitment.

Okay, that's enough about marriage. It's just an analogy, after all, and all analogies break down somewhere. So let's distill the point of the analogy as simply as possible: We have some precedent for self-denying commitment as a way of living despite personal uncertainty. Faith without belief may not look exactly like an arranged marriage. But it does offer us a vision of starting with commitment. It requires a reorientation of our cultural assumptions, no doubt. We're taught to start with doubt. We often slip into "Enlightenment thinking" without, ironically, thinking about or questioning Enlightenment thinking itself. Sometimes, doubt is appropriate and healthy, after all. We don't, and shouldn't, uncritically accept everything we're told. That's how credit card scams happen, folks.

But behind the basic thesis of this book is the opposite is sometimes true, too: Sometimes, it's appropriate and healthy to start with faith. Anselm did it and, in the long history of the Christian intellectual tradition, he's far from the only one. We may struggle with severe doubts or have trouble accepting every claim of the Christian tradition. But the way of commitment is available to us, nonetheless. That is the way of trust and faith.

The Struggle Is Real: Faith with Doubt and Hope

I'm a sucker for the Narnia stories. My favorite one is whichever I'm reading at the moment. But one of the underrated installments from the series is *The Silver Chair*. One of my favorite scenes, involving one of my favorite characters, from the whole series comes from this book. The character is Puddleglum, the Marshwiggle. What a guy. Puddleglum is the Eeyore of Narnia. He's a gloomy pessimist with low self-esteem. In a defining scene, perhaps even the climax of the book, Puddleglum and the three children are trapped in the witch's underworld. They are trapped, more specifically, by the witch's spell. The source of her enchantment is the fire in the fireplace. Entranced by the fire, the witch begins to convince the children the underworld is all there is. No "overworld." No Narnia. No sun, trees, or stars. No lions. No Aslan. It's all imaginary, she tells them. The spell swells and all hope seems lost. But our hero, the Marshwiggle, jumps on the fire and stamps it out. He turns to the witch and launches into an epic speech,

> "One word, Ma'am," he said, coming back from the fire; limping, because of the pain. "One word. All you've been saying is quite right, I shouldn't wonder. I'm a chap who always liked to know the worst and then put the best face I can on it. So I won't deny any of what you said. But there's one more thing to be said, even so. Suppose we have only dreamed, or made up, all those things— trees and grass and sun and moon and stars and Aslan himself. Suppose we have. Then all I can say is that, in that case, the made-up things seem a good deal more

important than the real ones. Suppose this black pit of a kingdom of yours is the only world. Well, it strikes me as a pretty poor one. And that's a funny thing, when you come to think of it. We're just babies making up a game, if you're right. But four babies playing a game can make a play-world which licks your real world hollow. That's why I'm going to stand by the play world. I'm on Aslan's side even if there isn't any Aslan to lead it. I'm going to live as like a Narnian as I can even if there isn't any Narnia. So, thanking you kindly for our supper, if these two gentlemen and the young lady are ready, we're leaving your court at once and setting out in the dark to spend our lives looking for Overland. Not that our lives will be very long, I should think; but that's a small loss if the world's as dull a place as you say."[4]

Don't you just want to stand up and applaud? With his epic speech, Puddleglum breaks the spell. But he doesn't do so with reasoned objections to the witch's claims. He says, in effect, he will commit to Narnia and to Aslan even without the certainty that they're there. He doubts but he realizes, anyway, the witch's underworld isn't worth living in. He chooses the way of hope.

The whole idea of faith without belief may seem like a farce. Why, after all, should I trust something if I don't have solid reasons for believing it? Why not continue in my agnosticism? The reason, I think, is hope. We intuitively recognize there is something in this world worth living for—worth even giving our lives for. Puddleglum puts voice to this idea so well. The witch's spell has them nearly convinced that there is no Aslan or Narnia. Despite their experiences with the lion and in that country, they can no longer say they believe in them. But, to Puddleglum, that is beside the point—or at least it's not the whole point. There is something deeper, stronger, than what our minds can believe that tells us something is *right, true, good, beautiful.*

Puddleglum isn't the only sidekick hero to put words to this. Let's keep with the Inkling fantasy world theme for a moment. At the end of *The Two Towers*, Frodo and Sam are separated from

4. Lewis, *Silver Chair*, 190–91.

the fellowship.[5] They are lost, battered, and broken. Frodo, despondent, utters, "I can't do this, Sam." In response, Sam gives a rousing speech. Near the end, he recognizes it doesn't always make sense. "Folk in those stories"—the great stories that really mattered—"were holding onto something," Sam says. Even when it looks like hope is lost and it doesn't make sense to go any further, they held onto something. Frodo, as exhausted and depressed as ever, asks, "What are we holding onto?" Sam insists, "That there's some good in this world, Mr. Frodo. And it's worth fighting for." Even Gollum is moved.

We've been duped by a witch's spell. In a secular age, belief no longer comes easy to us. There are forces in and around our world working, at every turn, against our belief in God. It should be no surprise that so many of us struggle to believe. We buy into subtle lies about the nature of reality, like "the cosmos is all there is" or "you should only believe what you can see, touch, feel." These lies are powerful. Their pull is strong. And many of us fall under their spell. Despite our doubt, despite our nonbelief, we need not give up hope. We need not surrender our faith. The novelist George Bernanos was onto something when he said faith is "90 percent doubt and 10 percent hope."[6] It's not so for everyone's faith. But he's right about one thing. Faith is compatible with doubt. Faith is compatible with severe doubt. We need not have all our intellectual ducks in a row to commit our lives to Jesus and live as faithful members of his church.

Bernanos, though, recognizes we need more than our doubt. Like Sam says, we've got to hold onto *something*. Through our doubts, we need hope more than ever. Hope is what Puddleglum and Sam are holding onto. The philosopher Yujin Nagasawa gives this kind of hope without belief a name: "'cosmic optimism,' according to which ultimately all is good on a cosmic scale."[7] Cosmic optimism is hope that there is some good in this world that's worth fighting for, even when we can't precisely name it. Nagasawa

5. Jackson, dir., *Two Towers*.
6. As quoted in Nagasawa, "Silence, Evil, and Shusaku Endo," 257.
7. Nagasawa, "Silence, Evil, and Shusaku Endo," 257.

clarifies that cosmic optimism is *not* confidence in our beliefs about the world but *an attitude of humility*. We can embrace the fact that the ultimate questions, and answers, stretch beyond our finite minds. Such an attitude can open new ways of seeing the world that embrace that deeper, stronger feeling in us that there is something *right, true, good, beautiful*. This is a disposition of hope.

Nagasawa and Bernanos illuminate faith without belief but we must press further. Even if it's true that faith doesn't require we have our intellectual ducks in a row, it must have an object. The apostle Paul helps fill this out for us. Paul realized the importance of hope amid struggle. More than most of us, Paul knew struggle and suffering. He'd lived it. He was often imprisoned and beaten for his faith. But he also realized he wasn't alone. This was no mere personal struggle. *All of creation* is groaning, he wrote, for a future redemption. And that future redemption is the source of our hopes. In wafting scents of faith without belief, Paul continues,

> For in hope we are saved. Now hope that is seen is not hope. For who hopes for what is seen? But if we hope for what we do not see, we wait for it with patience. Likewise, the Spirit helps us in our weakness for we do not know how to pray as we ought, but that very Spirit intercedes with sighs too deep for words. And God, who searches the heart, knows what is the mind of the Spirit, because the Spirit intercedes for the saints according to the will of God. (Romans 8:24–27)

In hope we are saved. We hope, he reminds us, in what we do not *see*. His use of "see" is striking. Obviously, we don't "see" God in a straightforward way. Whatever it means for me to "see" God, the experience is different than how I see my water bottle right now. But "see" goes beyond what we sense. It can also mean something like "know." In phrasing things this way, Paul seems to allow for some level of intellectual uncertainty, even about the object of our hope. But how can we move forward? In hope, we ask God for help. We turn not to better arguments, but to the Spirit of God. And the Spirit prays on our behalf, according to God's will. Paul makes room for our questions and doubts, but insists our hope is not in the vague, general, or ethereal. Our hope is in the one God of the universe who saves. Our hope is in God's redemption plan, enfleshed in the person of Jesus Christ, and personalized to each of us through the Holy Spirit. It should be no surprise, then, that Paul places hope alongside faith and love as the three Christian virtues (1 Corinthians 13:13). When we can't get to belief, hope is more than a suitable substitute. And it starts with asking for God's help—"Help my unbelief!"

In a long-lasting exchange of letters with C. S. Lewis, Sheldon Vanauken wrote of his struggles to believe. Like an earlier version of Lewis himself, Vanauken was a skeptic. He was attracted to Christianity, but found himself reluctant to commit. Despite Lewis's sharp, generous defense of the claims of Christianity, Vanauken simply struggled to get there. But in recounting his "encounter with light," Vanauken describes his conversion to Christianity to Lewis like this:

> I choose to believe in the Father, Son, and Holy Ghost—in Christ, my lord and my God. Christianity has the ring, the feel, of unique truth. Of essential truth. By it, life is made full instead of empty, meaningful instead of meaningless . . . A choice was necessary: and there is no certainty. One can only choose a side. So I—I now choose my side: I choose beauty; I choose what I love. But choosing to believe is believing. It's all I can do: choose. I confess my doubts and ask my Lord Christ to enter my life. I do not *know* God is, I do but say: Be it unto me according to Thy will. I do not affirm that I am without doubt, I do but ask for help, having chosen, to overcome it. I do but say, "Lord, I believe—help Thou my unbelief."[8]

Vanauken's expression of faith without belief is remarkable. For a secular age like our own, Vanauken need not be a blip on the radar but a possible path forward. In lieu of belief and in the struggle to believe, we might see commitment to Jesus as a viable option.

It should be clear by now I'm not recommending holding onto the vague "good" or "beautiful." Yes, our encounters with the true,

---

8. Vanauken, *Severe Mercy*, 99.

good, and beautiful can direct us toward God and, we'll soon find, are themselves encounters with God himself, even when we can't see it. But the vague "good" or "beautiful," as Vanauken realized, only make for good introductions to God. They cannot be that to which our faith is directed, at least not as we perceive them apart from God. In choosing beauty, in choosing love, Vanauken realized he was choosing Jesus. He was choosing God. He fell well short of the kind of certain belief we often associate with Christianity. But he found his path of faith without that belief.

Many years after Vanauken wrote the above letter to C. S. Lewis, my friend Ben stood in the waters of baptism and read the letter aloud. He'd read Vanauken's book only weeks earlier and Vanauken put a voice to Ben's experience better than he could do himself. Standing up to his waist in water and with a microphone in hand, Ben, like Vanauken, plainly admitted the tension in his life. He had severe doubts. He struggled to believe. But he was holding onto something. He was holding onto the hope offered in Jesus Christ. With the frantic father, he confessed his doubt and asked Jesus to help him with his unbelief. Ben was baptized into the church that day and chose a life committed to Jesus. Thanks be to God, the God who saves is faithful and will carry the work he started in Ben and Sheldon Vanauken to completion.

4

Christian Living for Nonbelievers

Faithful Living through Doubt

"She jumped up: she had but to keep that light in view and she must find the house. Her heart grew strong. Speedily, yet softly, she walked down the hill, hoping to pass the watching creature unseen. Dark as it was, there was little danger now of choosing the wrong road. And—which was most strange—the light that filled her eyes from the lamp, instead of blinding them for a moment to the object upon which they next fell, enabled her for a moment to see it, despite the darkness."

—GEORGE MACDONALD, *THE PRINCESS AND THE GOBLIN*

I'M A BASEBALL FAN and it's a grind. Yes, being a fan is a grind. The Major League season has 162 games per year. If your team is good, you get more games.[1] I read and sleep more in the offseason.

1. I'm a White Sox fan so I usually don't need to worry about that.

But imagine being a player. One game of baseball isn't as physically demanding as one game of basketball or football, of course. But playing *every day* takes a toll. Football and basketball players usually have several days in between games. For baseball players, it's sometimes just several hours. That's what makes consecutive games played streaks so impressive. Cal Ripken Jr. earned the title of baseball's iron man. He holds a record considered by many to be one of the few unbreakable records in baseball: he played 2,632 games in a row. With a 162-game season, that's *sixteen seasons* (and a month) without missing a *single game*. To put it in perspective, the longest streak in more recent memory belongs to Whit Merrifield, who played 553 games—oh, you know, just over two thousand games shy of Ripken's record. You've got to be tough for a streak like this, no doubt playing through all sorts of bumps, bruises, and sore limbs. Ripken took his streak into his late thirties. I'm in my early thirties and it takes me several days to recover from my weekly slow pitch softball games.[2]

Unsurprisingly, Ripken was well known for his work ethic. You don't churn out this kind of streak on accident. Some guys have trouble staying healthy for a few months. For others it feels like divine intervention if they stay healthy for two straight weeks. To do it for years, it takes focused training and a lot of it. That's the only way to survive a grind. Most people can survive one period or a spurt of activity, even if it's a lot. A few years ago, a former roommate of mine (the one with the Gollum voice) was getting married so he hosted a bachelor party. But his bachelor party wasn't a normal one. We called it "sports day." We look back on it with fondness and fatigue. It was, without question, the most exhausting day of my life. The shindig started on Friday night. All ten of us showed up at our friend's house for dinner followed by *hours* of ping pong. We finally went to sleep around 3 AM. The festivities began a few hours later. Then 10 AM seemed to come earlier than normal. We were divided into two teams of five and competed in six different sports. In order, we played volleyball, soccer, wiffleball, football,

2. At the time of writing this, I'm questionable for tonight's game because of a tumble I took last week. My three-game streak is now in jeopardy.

ultimate frisbee, and basketball. You get a bunch of competitive dudes together for a day and no one is taking it easy. We played, and played hard, all day with only a couple of meal breaks. But we survived. With little prior training, we endured rigorous athletic competition for twelve hours straight. We'll call it irrelevant that it took me nine days to recover.

"That'll preach," as they say. There's an important lesson here. With little work, we can achieve a lot in a little amount of time. We can run a sprint. We may be ill equipped and collapse afterward. But we could pull it off. We couldn't run a marathon. That takes sustained effort and training over time. Christian living is more like a marathon. High school church-campgoers are no doubt familiar with the "mountain top experience." It's what happens when you get caught up in the emotion of learning about and worshipping Jesus. It's a short spurt of warm, fuzzy, Jesus-loving feelings. But then you come back from camp. You go back to school. And rhythms and monotony of daily life take over. The excitement of camp passes and you're back to the daily grind. So it's one thing to talk about commitment without beliefs in the abstract, but it's another to go on with daily living as a Christian. It's one thing for lovers to exclaim "I'll love you forever" in a moment of passion, but it's quite another to live in a lifelong, faithful relationship. Christian living is difficult enough under any circumstances. But it's especially difficult when you have severe doubts about it all. What we need is Christian living for nonbelievers. We need stable practices that help us remain faithful even when our beliefs are unstable.

The Sunday School Answers: Prayer and Scripture

Sunday school answers get a bad rap. At least in Christian circles, it's common for a group leader to ask a spiritual question and, before anyone has a chance to answer, interject, "no Sunday school answers allowed." Fair enough. Sunday school answers get their reputation because they're simple. And, if my recollection of Sunday school when I was fifteen is any indication, rarely thought through. They are the answers you know you're *supposed* to give, not the ones you *want* to give. But sometimes Sunday school answers are the best answers. I'm going to pull back the curtain on my book writing and say I didn't want to write this section. Don't get me wrong: I wasn't avoiding Scripture or prayer. But when it comes to Christian practice, it's easy to write them off as boring. We're used to them. They're the Sunday school answers. So we're tempted to crowd them out in favor of fresh or edgier answers. We want to show we're smart or witty. But, simply put, any encouragement toward Christian living without prayer and Scripture is incomplete. Since the earliest Christians began worshiping Jesus as Lord, prayer and Scripture have played a central role in that worship. These historic spiritual disciplines have been the lifeblood of the church, pulsing through her veins and bringing life to all her body parts from the beginning. Christian believers understand each as genuinely relating to God. But what about when we doubt? How do we read Scripture? How do we pray?

We all read a lot. I read mostly theology and fiction books. Another friend of mine avoids nonfiction like the plague but reads a heavy diet of fiction and poetry. Another friend reads history and mysteries. Another friend doesn't read books and he wears it like a badge of pride (so I don't have to worry about him reading this). But even he still reads *a lot*. He reads social media posts and articles about basketball and conspiracy theories. Even if we don't consider ourselves readers, we're overrun with information and most of it comes in text form. And then there's the Bible in the middle of all this, competing for our reading eyes. The Bible is foundational for Christianity. One early church historian called Christianity a "bookish religion" for its almost obsessive production and preservation of written texts, especially Scripture.[3] The Christian Scripture includes texts received from pre-Jesus Israel (usually called the "Old Testament") as well as records and reflections on the life, death, and resurrection of Jesus Christ (or the "New Testament"). This is the foundation upon

3. Hurtado, *Destroyer of the gods.*

which all Christian theology, ethics, and philosophy is built. A *book* is central to the Christian life.

And yet the Bible resists categorization as merely a "book." For one, it's called "holy"—set apart or different. The Bible isn't like the other books I read or the articles about Kentucky basketball my friend reads. Christians confess the Bible as God-inspired or even God's own word. Christians through the centuries have disagreed on exactly how the Bible is God-inspired or what that even means, but they've all agreed this book is central to Christian living. But the Bible stands apart from other books in another way. While it's one cohesive unit, it's also a collection of writings from different authors, contexts, and genres. So I read theology and fiction but my friend reads history: the Bible includes all this (and more). Add it all up and you get a very complex book. For its simple message—Jesus is the embodiment of Israel's God who's come to make everything right again and install a regime that will never end—Scripture contains many complex layers. For this reason, disagreements about what the Bible teaches inspire intense conflicts and, ultimately, schism among Christian denominations today.

So perhaps it shouldn't surprise us that the Bible, maybe more than anything else, invites questions about God and the Christian life from college students. In my college ministry work, I've received more questions about something the Bible says than other topic (Christian ethics or philosophy or God's existence). And I don't think it's close. When you go to seminary, people seem to think you're an expert in the Bible: "What do you think about Hezekiah 12:47?," I'm often asked.[4] But even over the last decade, the complexion of Bible questions has changed. Instead of pointing to a particular verse the complaint seems to be more general. Why is it all so unclear? Christian denominations flow out of conflicting interpretations like water from the Nile. Wouldn't it be so much easier if the Bible was clear, and then we could all just get along? Wouldn't it be easier if Jesus said, "this is a metaphor and this isn't" or Paul added, "this is for the Corinthian church

4. Don't look up Hezekiah 12:47 yourself.

only and not every church from now until the end of time"? The Bible is a messy book not only because it's stained with sin. It's a messy book because it's complex and sometimes difficult to follow. It often confounds our expectations about who God is or how he should act. And during periods of intense doubts, reading the Bible feels like a risk. Will we do more harm than good? Should doubters or nonbelievers even bother with the Bible?

They should. The struggles involved with reading Scripture are precisely *why* they should bother. Consider other books we read or even movies we watch. Sure, we'll often enjoy simple, straightforward fun reads—*The Da Vinci Code* is hard to put down, isn't it? But the books that stick with us ask more from us. My favorite books aren't breezy beach reads. I sometimes read those, too, but they dart in and out of my life so quickly they're easy to forget. The ones that stick with me are long, complicated books which ask difficult questions even if they don't give clear answers. *Madame Bovary*, *The Brothers Karamazov*, and *East of Eden*, to scratch a few examples off the top, tell human stories about the struggle with sin, doubt, and God's grace. They may not use any of those words. The themes are rarely, if ever, explicitly mentioned. But they're there. Sometimes you only see them in the struggle. The book lodges itself in your mind and heart. It's unforgettable. And you're pulled back to the story to let it work on you more. The Bible is like that, only on steroids. You can peel layer after layer of rich themes relevant to our lives, but they aren't always sitting there on the surface. We might have to read a verse, a passage, a book several times before it sticks. And even then we won't have plumbed the depths of what it offers. We never will.

Despite all its rich complexity, the Bible is also simple. During the Reformation, one of the flashpoints was the place of Scripture in our churches and theology. The Reformers cry was "*Sola Scriptura*"—"Scripture alone." This is sometimes taken to mean we should only read the Bible and not give two hoots what the tradition thinks. But this clearly isn't true for the early Reformers. They cared *a lot* about the tradition and saw wisdom in receiving and submitting to it. But they also wanted to preserve the plain, simple message of Scripture. The hypothetical man on an island could read the Bible in his language and understand some simple truths: God created him, he fails to meet the standard God's creation sets for him, but because of what Jesus Christ does for him he can be saved by his trust in Jesus. That, after all, is the good news message of hope for the world. The Bible perfectly walks the line between simplicity and complexity: You don't need a PhD in theology and literature, an extensive knowledge of Greek, or to be a spiritual master to read and be changed by the message, but even with all this you'll only scratch the surface of the riches it has to offer. In all its simplicity and complexity, the Bible invites us further into God's world and his plans for our lives. It challenges us and leaves us with questions. But through the mist it paints a clearer picture of Jesus and, therefore, of God. Nonbelievers can embrace the struggle.

I can't resist another baseball reference. You should be used to it by now. *A League of Their Own* tells the true story of women's baseball, a replacement league during World War II.[5] Near the end of the movie, star player Dottie Henson (Geena Davis) tells manager Jimmy Dugan (Tom Hanks) her plans to quit baseball, move away, and start a family with her husband. While she's hiding behind the wall of her family, Dugan can tell there's more to the story. He presses her until she admits, "It just got too hard." Dugan responds, "It's supposed to be hard. If it wasn't hard, everyone would do it. The hard . . . is what makes it great." Whether it's playing professional baseball or running a marathon or climbing a mountain or watching all three extended editions of *Lord of the Rings* in the same day, we're compelled by hard things. We're drawn to challenges which push us to our limits. We enjoy the accomplishment itself, but it's the hard that's great.

Scripture and prayer can be like that. I've just made a big deal out of the simplicity of Scripture and prayer is no different. The simple, sincere prayer of the lost person is one of the most beautiful and profound things uttered by humans. But, like Scripture, prayer can be a struggle. There's an ease and simplicity to it, so that anyone could do it. I'd start by saying simply, "Give it a go." And prayer is

5. Penny Marshall, dir., *A League of Their Own*.

often intimate and personal, so I don't know what else to add. But I will add that it can be a challenge, too. It can be hard. But that's one of the things that makes it great. For doubters and nonbelievers, it may be difficult to muster up the piety to pray from your own heart. What do I say? How do I ask for things? How do I ask for forgiveness? Are there good and bad ways to pray?

God will always hear our sincere cries but that doesn't mean there aren't better or worse ways to pray. When his disciples asked Jesus to teach them to pray, he didn't rebuke them and say, "There's no right way to pray, so just say whatever's on your mind." No, he said, "This is how you do it." He gave them a template as well as a specific prayer to pray. Of course, it doesn't mean every prayer we pray must be a recitation of the Lord's Prayer. But this prayer can be a place to turn for guidance. Historically, when the church yearns for the right words at the right time, she's known she can turn to the Lord's Prayer when she doesn't have the right words to pray. In addition to this prayer, many ancient prayers of the church have been preserved. Drawn from Scripture itself, the so-called Jesus prayer is simply, "Lord Jesus Christ, Son of the living God, have mercy on me a sinner." This simple prayer is meant to be repeated, over and over again, working on our hearts in unseen ways. If you're stuck in prayer, these can be a good place to start. They are wells to draw from when we don't know where else to find water. When prayer is hard, we can say this prayer. By praying with others—especially our Lord—we'll learn how to pray.

Scripture and prayer are Sunday school answers because they are the *right* answers. Sometimes the obvious paths are the best ones. But we can't dismiss the fact that, for many, Scripture and prayer are a catalyst for doubt instead of a remedy. The complexities of Scripture or silence of God often invite doubts, not rebuff them. But, as frustrating and challenging as it can be, it's worth embracing what's hard. It's worth embracing the struggle. We can, along the way, learn from others. Like anything, practice makes . . . maybe not perfect, but usually pretty good. Sometimes reading the Bible and praying are like breaking in a new baseball glove. It feels unnatural and unhelpful at first, but the more you use it the better it gets.

Nevertheless, chances are nonbelievers and doubters have given these a shot. They're the Sunday school answers, so that's usually the first place you look. If doubt and nonbelief remain a struggle, it's worth asking: What's next? What else can I do?

Images of Jesus: Knowing God through Others

The silence of God can be crushing. That's why prayer, especially, is often a challenge for nonbelievers. Why doesn't God speak? Why doesn't he make himself more obvious? We're back to our medieval knight, looking for his next move. But hearing God is difficult if we don't know where and how to listen. If we expect God to write a message in the clouds or audibly speak over a cosmic intercom, we're setting ourselves up for disappointment. It's not because God isn't interested in relationship with us. But we can and should recognize how our expectations of God are influencing what we perceive as a lack of relationship. To be attentive to God's activity, we must learn the right kind of attention. Where do we turn?

Maybe another Tom Hanks movie reference can help. In *The Terminal*, Viktor (Tom Hanks) is an Eastern European refugee stuck in a New York City airport.[6] He's stuck because Viktor's country succumbed to a coup while he was on an airplane bound for the USA. Because of legal complications, Viktor can neither return to his home country nor enter the USA. Caught in the longest layover of his life, Viktor does the only thing he can do. He adapts to life in an airport. He figures out how to eat for cheap, he makes friends, and thrives despite fierce opposition from the airport administration. His friends especially help him along the way. Enrique is a food service worker and janitor. Dolores is a security guard assigned to screening immigration cases. Despite her exasperated attempts to tell the confused, non-English-speaking Viktor he cannot enter the US, she can't help but feel a great deal of sympathy for him. So, every day he comes to get the stamp he

---

6. Steven Spielberg, dir., *The Terminal* (2004).

so badly needs, and every day she turns him down. Through their daily interactions, they form a friendship.

Meanwhile, Enrique is madly in love with Dolores. The problem is: Dolores knows nothing of Enrique. She doesn't even know he exists! Enrique works in the shadows of the airport. He fears an overt profession of his love would end in rejection, thereby lowering the likelihood of any relationship with Dolores. If introducing himself out of the blue would backfire, what's Enrique to do? He notices Viktor is chummy with Dolores. So, he hatches a plot. He offers Viktor a deal: In exchange for food, Viktor will speak to Dolores during his daily visits about a "mystery man" who loves her. Confirming Enrique's fears, Dolores is initially uninterested in Viktor's mystery man. But Viktor's gentle persistence and persuasion slowly softens her heart toward this mystery man. In the end, Enrique proposes, Dolores says yes, and Viktor finally makes it out of the airport. It is a movie, after all.

What does *The Terminal* teach us about a relationship with God? Here's one thing it makes plain: Sometimes to woo another you must work in the shadows. We know it doesn't *always* work like that. You might "meet cute" (am I using that right?) and it's love at first sight. At least, that's what the movies tell us. But, sometimes, the circumstances of the situation require another plan of action. I get it: When you love someone and they're oblivious to your existence, there's a fine line between "loving" and "creepy." But love stories are filled with examples of forbidden or unknowing love. God's love can be like that toward some people. We know God loves everyone. That's the Sunday school answer. But some people don't love God back. They might object to God's "hiddenness" because God is not obvious to them. But God's "hiddenness" may well be an act of his love. Among other things, sin and secularity create conditions in which belief is difficult. In response, why couldn't God work in the shadows?

Of course, he can't stay in the shadows. In *The Terminal*, Enrique sees his way out: Viktor. To pursue his true love, he uses Viktor to grow closer to Dolores. It's not a bad idea. In fact, it's an idea we've likely had ourselves. The basic idea is this: We're more likely to respond positively to someone if someone else we trust introduces us. Let's look at an example. Suppose Charles meets a stranger, Wilcox, at a party. They bump into each other at the punch bowl and have a chat. Maybe they hit it off. But most likely, they'll have a polite little conversation and that'll be that. But let's change the details of the story a bit. Suppose, instead of meeting at the punch bowl, their mutual friend Cordelia gets involved. They both trust Cordelia. She grabs Charles by the arm, marches him over to Wilcox, and says, "Oh, you two simply must meet. You'd be the best of friends. You both love cricket and reading Jane Austen, for one." It doesn't guarantee they'll hit it off. But how much more likely is it that Charles and Wilcox will become friends? How much more likely that they give it a go and meet for tea after the party? That's the role Viktor plays for Enrique and Dolores. His introduction is effective because he knows them both and they both trust him. Dolores is more receptive to the "mystery man" because it's Viktor who's telling her about him. Viktor's descriptions and encouragement seal the deal.

If God's dealings with humans in Scripture are any indication, we can say God often works through people to accomplish his purposes. God is a working-through-people kind of God.[7] When he creates the world, he puts humans at the center to bear his image and be his representatives on earth. When humanity falls and needs redemption, God chooses a people group, Israel, through whom he'd reveal himself to the rest of the world. God sends prophets, priests, and kings to represent him and direct his people down his paths. Then, in the culmination of God's redemption plan, he enters his creation as a human man. Jesus Christ is *the* Prophet, Priest, and King. And when Jesus ascends into heaven, he tells his followers, "*You* will be my witnesses in Jerusalem, in all Judea and Samaria, and to the ends of the earth" (Acts 1:8). From creation through redemption and to the ends

---

7. The Bible scholar N. T. Wright called God a "*dianthropic*" (from Greek "*dia*" meaning "through" and "*anthropos*" meaning "person") God. God primarily reveals himself to people through other people, was his point. Wright made this comment in an unpublished lecture, but it's used here with his permission.

of the earth, God's works *through* people to accomplish his purposes. Even when they mess up, God doesn't scratch the plan. He continues to work through people. Because God is a work-through-people kind of God.

What does it look like when God works through people? It may be helpful to start way back, in the beginning. When God creates humans as his images, he does something unique. A contemporary, rival creation narrative like the Mesopotamian *Enuma Elish*, for example, portrays the creation of humankind as an afterthought and humanity's role as servanthood to the gods. Genesis tells a very different story. God creates humans as the culmination of creation and defines them as bearers of his very image. This is important not only for humanity's relationship with God, but for our relationship with the rest of the created order. Biblical scholars have offered a lot of insight into what it means to be created in another's image. When we think of an "image," we typically think of a visual depiction of something. But there's more to image-bearing than looking like God. It is a vocation. It is a calling.

A helpful way to see what it means to image God is to understand it as both representational and representative.[8] If something is *representational*, it resembles something or someone in some way. But the *representative* component refers to vocation. It's a responsibility to act in God's stead. Okay, but those sound a little too similar. Consider an analogy. I've always looked like my dad. When I was young, a week could hardly go by without someone commenting, "You look just like your father." I had to come up with some witty retort, like "is that supposed to be a compliment?" And I must say, pictures of us as kids are uncanny. So, I could say I *representationally* image my father because I look like him. But I might also image him in another way. When I was a little older, I was sometimes tasked with looking after my younger sister while Mom and Dad went away for a while. My dad might say something like, "Look after your sister, and make sure she doesn't watch MTV." I'm still under the authority of my father, but

8. This helpful framing is J. Richard Middleton's in Middleton, *Liberating Image*, 88.

while my parents are away, I am acting on his behalf. He has commissioned me to look after my sister as if he were doing it himself. This could include, even, punishing my sister if she tried to sneak some MTV after I'd explicitly told her not to watch it. So, I could say I *representatively* image my father by acting in his stead.

When we were created in God's image, we were created to representationally and representatively image God. Of course, we fail miserably. It's as if God crafted a beautiful statue and we tossed a bucket of mud and mire on our own heads. Clearly, God's image in us needs cleansing. And it's cleansing we're offered. The apostle Paul makes it clear we're still to think of ourselves as image bearers. But the image is only properly restored through Jesus Christ. He is "*the* image of the invisible God" (Colossians 1:15). He says elsewhere those predestined by God are being "conformed to the image of his Son" (Romans 1:29). Paul is not contradicting Genesis. But he is radically reframing it in light of who Christ is and what Christ has accomplished. One biblical scholar says the image is a "family resemblance"[9] while another calls the image "functional" because "believers are called even in the present to represent God within creation and to cooperate with God to bring redemption to that creation."[10] In short, God doesn't give up on humans because they mess up and Jesus steps in. Our role remains central.

Let's return to our medieval knight in *The Seventh Seal*. Though his squire goes with him, the knight's travel home feels solitary. He's stoic and quiet. He's trapped in his thoughts, unable to constrain his doubts. But there's a turn when he comes across a lovely young family. The young husband and wife are traveling actors with their young child. Despite the apocalyptic surroundings of the Crusades and the plague ravishing Europe, the family emits a simple joy and contentment. In one scene, they're reclining outside, overlooking nature, snacking on fruit. They invite the knight to recline with them. He noticeably comes alive. He says, smiling,

9. Mounce, *Romans*, 189.
10. Jacob, *Conformed to the Image of His Son*, 10.

> I shall remember this moment: the silence, the twilight,
> the bowl of strawberries, the bowl of milk. Your faces in
> the evening light . . . I shall carry this memory carefully
> in my hands as if it were a bowl brimful of fresh milk. It
> will be a sign to me, and a great sufficiency.

Though he may not name it so, the knight catches a glimpse of something good and beautiful and, therefore, of God. The experience is not necessarily religious. But it is a "sign" and "sufficiency" for the knight. He experiences God's gifts of nature and people and, in doing so, receives a foretaste of God's eternal joys. In the end, when the knight faces Death for the last time, he faces him in prayer. Who knows if his experience with this family was the grace given by God to sustain him?

We may not always like it, but the story God is telling puts humans at the center. Christian living is imperfect without others. Christians have long recognized the importance of community. The Christian life is difficult. But it's far more difficult when we go at it alone. When many people talk about Christian living, they think of spiritual disciplines we often do alone: prayer, reading our Bible, fasting. Those are fantastic things, critical for Christian living. But even those practices can and should be practiced together. The Christian life is life *together*. When we fail to see that, we'll fail to see God.

Face-to-face: Jesus in the Church and Least of These

Let's rewind back to Doubting Thomas. Thomas—like us, like the medieval knight—looks for something tangible. He wants to know. He wants to see. He wants to touch. Thomas needs to see Jesus face-to-face before he can really believe it. Nonbelievers and doubters are like Thomas. We want to see Jesus face-to-face. We see ourselves in Thomas. But we can take heart. Even though Thomas gets the reputation as the doubter, the guy who didn't have enough faith, Jesus doesn't rebuke Thomas. After Thomas's profession of doubt, Jesus appears to him. He says, "Put your finger here and see my hands. Reach out your hand and put it in my side. Do not doubt but believe" (John 20:27). Notice the order. Jesus doesn't first say "do not doubt but believe," then give him the opportunity to touch him. Jesus first says "touch" then "believe." Thomas's demand to see Jesus face-to-face is answered. We who doubt today may think, "Well, that's all well and good for Thomas, but what about me? Can I not meet Jesus face-to-face? Can I not touch his body and blood?" According to Christianity, we can—if we listen to Jesus himself. Jesus gives us at least two ways to meet him face-to-face.

Jesus talked a lot about judgment. Judgement passages like these often make us squirm because we wonder, "Where do I fit in?" Perhaps no passage invites this discomfort like Matthew 25. Jesus says,

> Then the king will say to those at his right hand, "Come, you that are blessed by my Father, inherit the kingdom prepared for you from the foundation of the world; for I was hungry and you gave me food, I was thirsty and you gave me something to drink, I was a stranger and you welcomed me, I was naked and you gave me clothing, I was sick and you took care of me, I was in prison and you visited me." Then the righteous will answer him, "Lord, when was it that we saw you hungry and gave you food, or thirsty and gave you something to drink? And when was it that we saw you a stranger and welcomed you, or naked and gave you clothing? And when was it that we saw you sick or in prison and visited you?" And the king will answer them, "Truly I tell you, just as you did it to one of the least of these who are members of my family, you did it to me." (Matthew 25:34–40).

Startlingly, Jesus identifies himself with those he calls the "least of these"—the hungry, the stranger, the unclothed, and the imprisoned. Perhaps it shouldn't surprise us, given the rest of Jesus's life and the way he often aligned himself with the least of these. But this passage runs counter to many of our intuitions about where Jesus is found. More tragically, it runs counter to the kind of people with whom the church is sometimes associated. But we can't escape the conclusion that Jesus identifies himself with such people, to such an extent that spending time with "the least of these" is spending time with Jesus himself. When we feed the hungry, visit the imprisoned, or care for the sick, we meet Jesus face-to-face.

A couple of dangers lurk. First and most importantly, our temptation is to instrumentalize the "least of these" and see them only as means to an end. I can't only love others *so that* I'll meet Jesus. It's safe to say that if we do that then we've missed the point. Every person deserves our love and attention because they bear God's image and are objects of God's love. That is enough. But the point is we can hardly complain about not meeting Jesus face-to-face if we ignore (or worse) the least of these. It's hardly surprising we struggle with God's hiddenness. A second danger, however, is we might expect warm, fuzzy feelings of God's presence when we meet the hungry, imprisoned, and sick. Anyone that's spent any time in these communities know that's not always the case. Mother Teresa is an excellent example. Despite her several years of working among the poorest of the poor in India, she also struggled with God's silence.[11] She often found the work grueling and difficult. But just because we don't *feel* God's presence doesn't mean God isn't present. We may not yet understand how God is present to us in such moments but, one day, we will.

Jesus meets us face-to-face in the least of these. But he gives us an even more intimate way to meet him. He extends to us the same opportunity he extends to Thomas: to touch his body and blood. Before his brutal death, Jesus gathered his disciples to celebrate the traditional Passover meal. But these Jewish men, who'd eaten this meal since they were kids, quickly realized this wasn't your typical Passover meal. Jesus passed them bread and wine:

> While they were eating, Jesus took a loaf of bread, and after blessing it he broke it, gave it to the disciples, and said, "Take, eat; this is my body." Then he took a cup, and after giving thanks he gave it to them, saying, "Drink from it, all of you; for this is my blood of the covenant, which is poured out for many for the forgiveness of sins." (Matthew 26:26–28).

11. Teresa, *Mother Teresa.*

This Passover meal was central to their Jewish identity. It told the story of God's redemption and invited participants into that story. But Jesus reconfigured the meal around himself and, specifically, his death. Through bread and wine, he invites his followers to receive his body and blood. Later reflecting on the power of this meal, the apostle Paul calls it a "sharing" or "participation" in the body and blood of Jesus Christ. Like the Jewish Passover meal before it, this communion meal invites participants into the story of God's redemption.

If you follow politics, you'll sometimes hear an issue called a "third rail"—first applied to social security—because it's so charged and divisive as to be untouchable. On an electric railway system, the third rail splits the other two tracks and is charged with a powerful electric current. Whoever touches it usually dies by electrocution. Theology has its third rails, too. The meal Jesus gave us—sometimes called the Eucharist, Communion, or the Lord's Supper—is a good example. Historical and contemporary theology is full of debates about what this meal is or how it works. Whatever denomination or tradition you're familiar with almost certainly has a doctrinal statement about it. But—as charged as this issue is—we can't avoid it. This celebratory meal has been central to Christian worship since Jesus instituted it and we ignore it at our peril.

Jesus said it best: "This is my body . . . this is my blood." There's a simplicity to it. There's a lot more we could ask or say: What does he mean by this? What's going on physically? Is it still bread and wine? As a theologian, questions like these are hard to resist but, at risk of electrocution, let's set them aside. However you answer these questions, one thing is clear: Jesus himself invited us to see him in these elements. We don't need comprehensive answers to these questions to see Jesus. As C. S. Lewis points out, "The command, after all, was 'Take, Eat,' not 'Take, Understand.'"[12] We can, through the bread and wine, *touch* and *receive* Jesus. We're invited into his story of redemption. And it's the most appropriate place to bring our doubts. When the communion meal

12. Lewis, *Letters to Malcolm*, 104.

is served, we can almost hear the voice of Jesus, "Put your finger here and see my hands. Reach out your hand and put it in my side. Do not doubt but believe" (John 20:27). Taking our cue from Thomas, we can say in return, "My Lord and my God!"

Once again, we may not *feel* anything when we receive the elements. Our doubts may not disappear the first time we receive. But we're invited, like Thomas, to touch Jesus and see him face-to-face. Our lack of belief need not stop us from confessing Jesus as Lord. We may not find this Jesus meal sufficient for belief. But what the communion table should preach, above all, is God's grace. It's not *ultimately* "up to us." At my church, we receive the bread and wine kneeling with our hands outstretched. We *receive* God's body and blood, having not earned it ourselves. The small actions of kneeling and receiving with our hands outstretched is meant to enact our salvation: Christ gives to us, and we receive. We participate in Christ's death in this meal because we tangibly see, touch, taste what God does for us. In the words of the psalmist, "we taste and see that the Lord is good" (Psalm 34:8).

Faith *With* Belief

As a huge fan of *The West Wing*, I can't help thinking in political examples. It's likely no surprise to anyone reading this that we Americans vote for our elected representatives, even the leader of our country. We're not a monarchy. So we're often called a democracy or democratic. But political nerds are quick to point out we're not, strictly speaking, a democracy. We're a republic. That's what Benjamin Franklin was supposed to have said when asked what kind of government they created: "A republic, if you can keep it." Our republic often has the *feel* of democracy. Every four years, we vote on who will lead our country. Occasionally, amendments to our state constitution will be on the ballot, too. But we typically don't vote on laws. Our lawmakers, as our representatives, make the laws and we're expected to obey them, even if we don't agree with them. In the words of Toby Ziegler, "Laws don't work like that . . . We don't ask for a show of hands." For all our democratic

tendencies, we're not a straightforward democracy. Our representatives do the governing on our behalf.

Representatives—big surprise—are expected to *represent*
their constituents. The representatives we elect in my home state
of Kentucky should, when all is working properly, represent the
needs, concerns, and interests of Kentuckians. But once we elect
a representative, there is a sense in which governing is out of our
hands. And that's usually a good thing. I can't be expected to keep
up with every intricacy of every law. Our representatives—in an
ideal world that, sadly, probably doesn't describe reality—can
read bills, know them well, and vote accordingly. But there is a
downside. Our representative may believe something we don't.
They may fight for policies we detest. It's an interesting dynamic
because my representative does things on my behalf, but I don't
always approve. So the situation is one in which we can say things
about a group which doesn't apply to many individuals in the
group. For example—and I'm doing my best not to touch any third
rails but, since everything feels like a third rail these days, here
it goes—when Kentucky's legislature and governor defends gun
ownership, we can say: "Kentucky believes in gun rights." But that
doesn't apply to every individual person in Kentucky. Many people
in Kentucky would like to pass much stricter gun laws, including
taking guns away from every person, for example.

But let's not get sidetracked by the politics. The point I want
to make isn't political at all. The point is representatives can believe
or act *on behalf of the group*. In many cases, the representative's
actions or believes will not reflect some individuals in the group.
Nevertheless, those dissenting individuals are still caught up in
the beliefs and actions of the wider community. It may sound
strange to talk about groups having beliefs. We might think only
people have beliefs and groups, obviously, aren't persons. But we
regularly talk in ways that assume the opposite. A group believes
and acts beyond what applies to the sum of its parts. Consider
statements like "the committee determined wrongdoing on the
part of the CEO," "the fanbase thinks the general manager is bad,"
or "the team was furious at the referee." We can make sense of all

these statements, even though we recognize they probably don't apply to every member of the group. Even so, everyone in the group is somehow caught up in the beliefs of the group because he or she is part of it.

Okay, that's a lot of talk about groups. What's the point? It's not a perfect analogy, but here it goes: The church is a group that believes and acts. This point is probably made clearest through a church's creeds and confessions. In my church, we "confess our faith in the words of the Nicene Creed." Every week, we all stand and recite the creed together, "I believe in God, the Father Almighty, maker of heaven and earth . . . I believe in Jesus Christ, his only Son our Lord . . . I believe in the Holy Spirit, the Lord, the giver of Life . . ." The Nicene Creed and its older, shorter cousin the Apostles' Creed are short confessions summarizing some of the basic beliefs of the church. Either in their weekly worship or implicitly, many churches believe what's recorded in these statements. When communally confessed, they invite all participants to say, "I believe . . ." But suppose my friend Ben joined our church. Could Ben, in good conscience, say "I believe?" Could Ben make this confession? Can he rightly, truly, or honestly say, "*I* believe in God . . ."?

Because the creed begins with "I," we're tempted to see the creed as an individual confession of faith. If that's true, Ben might struggle to make it through the first few words. But that's not the way the church has always seen her confession of belief. We tend to see everything through the lens of our own individuality. But the ancients who compiled these creeds we're not so individually inclined. Commenting on the Apostles' Creed, Ben Myers says an emphasis on "I" misses the point.[13] The creed specifically *isn't* merely some individual confession. In the words of the Rich Mullins song appropriately titled *Creed*, "I did not make it, no, it is making me, it the very truth of God and not the invention of any man." When we read the creed, we're reading a script given to us. It's handed down. We only receive and confess. It's the *church's* confession in which we participate. So Myers says simply, "Who is the 'I' that speaks when

13. Myers, *Apostles' Creed*, 9–11.

we make that confession? It is the body of Christ." He later adds, "In confessing the faith of the church, I allow my own individual 'I' to become part of the 'I' of the body of Christ."

When we understand the creed as the church's confession in which we participate, we can see clearer how doubters and nonbelievers fit in. In reciting creeds, the church is not a bunch of individuals making statements about what they as individuals believe. We are confessing, rather, as one, united body of Christ. The church believes as one unit. When we submit to her and participate in her confession, there's a sense in which we allow the church to be our representative. We allow the church to believe on our behalf. Our individual beliefs may sometimes be misaligned with her. But, in a recognition of our own weakness, doubt, or nonbelief, we plead, "Help my unbelief!" Through the beliefs of the church, Jesus gives space for our doubts and nonbelief. The communal confession of the church— displayed most clearly but not exclusively in her historical creeds and confessions—is an opportunity for doubters to share in the conviction of belief. By the Holy Spirit's power, the church is *one body* and Christ is the head of this body. It's all mystical and mysterious, like Paul said. But, with our faith firmly planted in Jesus, we can say with the great confession of the church, "I believe!"

I've talked much about "faith without belief," but maybe that's not quite right. Or at least we should add an asterisk. Yes, our personal and individual struggles to believe can culminate in personal faith without personal belief. But when we commit and submit to Christ and his church, we allow the church to believe on our behalf. Because we're joined to Christ by God's Spirit, we share in these beliefs just as much as anyone else. With eyes to see, we'll see these beliefs as our own, thanks to Christ's working in us. If that's right, faith without belief turns out *not* to be *without* belief at all. We have faith *with* belief. Our faith in Jesus Christ and commitment to his church allows us to share in the beliefs given by his grace alone. Thanks be to God.

Conclusion

LET'S RETURN TO WHERE we started: with Ben. At the time of writing this, I had breakfast with Ben a few days ago. We're only a few months removed from Ben's baptism. He's involved with his church. He's learning how to live the Christian life. But now begins the grind. It's time for Ben to start his own Ripken-esque streak of faithful, Christian living. Sometimes you go 0-4, but suiting up is still important. Ben is on the right path. He started on the path of faith without belief but, if I'm right, his path will lead to faith *with* belief one way or the other.

And now we come to a fact you've likely known from the beginning: Ben's story is rare. There aren't many conversion stories like Ben's. The far more common path is what some call "deconstruction." In popular Christian discourse, "deconstructing faith" is the move to question, doubt, and rethink given Christian beliefs. While it's often shrouded in pseudo-philosophical language, "deconstructing faith" is typically little more than disillusionment with a religious upbringing. Sometimes, the result is mild. Maybe you've rethought your Baptist upbringing in favor of Presbyterianism. Okay, that's one thing. But it can go in more extreme directions. "Deconstruction" might also lead to a rejection of all your previously held religious beliefs. It might land people in agnosticism or atheism or the ever-vague "spiritual-but-not-religious" ideology that preys on our universalist impulses. It's a tempting path for a secular age. But too few "deconstructors" consider a path of faith without belief. Too few see their doubt, insecurity, and uncertainty as a path for growth in God.

One of the most remarkable stories in Scripture is Jacob wrestling with God. Yes, you read that right. In the middle of the night, Jacob wrestles a man until dawn. The man, with a touch of a finger, puts Jacob's hip out of joint. Jacob knows whoever he's wrestling is no mere man. After insisting on the man's blessing, the man tells him he'll no longer be called Jacob but Israel because "you have striven with God and with humans, and have prevailed" (Genesis 32:28). The man blessed Jacob and left. Jacob said, "I have seen God face-to-face, and yet my life is preserved" (Genesis 32:30). Scholars debate whether the man Jacob wrestled with truly God incarnate or an angel, but the point remains: Jacob has wrestled, "striven," with God and—more remarkable still—he has "prevailed." Jacob isn't alone. Job "wrestles" with God in another sense. Through all the immense suffering God allows him, Job has little else to do but to contend with God. Job brings his sufferings before him, distraught and confused. He's acted in righteousness and yet God still afflicts him. He cries, "Does he not see my ways, and number all my steps? . . . Oh, that I had one to hear me! Here is my signature! let the Almighty answer me!" As with Jacob, the remarkable thing is God does answer him. Job stands up to God, complains, and *lives*. Like Thomas after them, God does not shut out our cries of confusion, frustration, or doubt. God lets us wrestle with him. When we do, we, like Jacob, prevail. "Deconstruction" is exactly the wrong path when we're faced with doubt or disillusionment. The much better path forward is to contend, to wrestle, to strive, with God.

Everybody's story is different. Everyone comes to God with a unique set of feelings, thoughts, and concerns. Personally, I still relate to Ben. Most weeks, I stand to confess my faith in the creed and I believe it. I confidently say, "I believe . . ." and I'm happy to say the "I" applies to the church *and* to me personally. But, as with anyone who struggles with doubt, some weeks I need help. I pray to Jesus, "Help my unbelief!" I need his church to believe for me when I'm too weak. I'm eternally grateful (literally) Jesus does not turn me away. He welcomes me to touch his body and blood, so I may believe again. I suspect many in the pews can, like me, relate to Ben. When we swim in the waters of doubt, the church can be a feeding ground for sharks. The church, after all, isn't perfect. Far from it. Just as often as showing us Jesus, it can turn us away from him. The church, for many, is the *source* of their disillusionment and doubt, not an antidote. The only certain antidote is faith. The best path forward is trust in God and in Jesus Christ. There is grace upon grace for our failures and struggles. Even when we can't see it, we can hope in what we do not see.

If anyone reads this, I'm sure I'll be accused, if only in some readers' minds, of downplaying the importance of belief. Before signing off, I want to respond to this accusation. In at least one sense, I can only say: guilty as charged. As I experience it in some expressions of the church today, "belief" feels very overplayed. Explicitly or implicitly, the message seems to be: What it means to be a Christian is to believe that Jesus was God, died for your sins, and resurrected—or whatever denominational variation on this you'd like to add. But this *must* be wrong. After all, even the demons "believe" (James 2:19). Belief is not unimportant, but neither should it be our primary focus. It cannot be, that is, the standard by which we deem people valid participants in the church or, worse, worthy of God's grace. Throughout his ministry on earth, Jesus welcomed children, the lame, the crippled. Does Jesus not also welcome the cognitively impaired? Does Jesus not also welcome those who, through no fault of their own, physically *cannot* believe? Indeed, he does—I suspect such people are not only welcome in God's kingdom but surpass us all for their unparalleled ability to *trust*. For some of God's image bearers, trust is all they can do. We have it on good authority: "The pure in heart will see God."

But neither do I want to make belief unimportant or, worse, irrelevant. In chapter 2, I quoted Alistair Kee, who said in 1971, "ours is an age of faith, but not belief."[1] Kee hit the nail on the head and recognized the challenges for the gospel in a secular age. Many of Kee's emphases are my own: the emphasis of faith as primarily an act of trust, the recognition that faith is compatible

1. Kee, *Way of Transcendence*, ix.

with nonbelief, and the like. But Kee goes too far. He says he speaks to a culture for which "it is impossible for them to believe in God."[2] In response, what he attempts is "a viable way of reinterpreting Christianity so that secular faith in Christ is possible." This, it seems to me, gets the order wrong. Our culture shouldn't "reinterpret" the gospel to fit ourselves or our culture, but we should reinterpret our culture to fit the gospel. In this book, I've tried to present a viable path forward for those of us in a secular age who struggle to believe. But this path is straight through the power of the gospel and traditional Christian belief. The beliefs are true and the backbone of Christian faith. Faith without belief is, if nothing else, a concession to our weakness. It's a way the gospel's power penetrates our sin and secularity.

While my separation of faith and belief might, at points, seem clean and easy, it is not so. Separating faith and belief is like separating oil and water. The emphasis of the New Testament use of "belief" or "faith" is trust and allegiance, but that doesn't mean belief—in the thinking sense—is altogether absent. What we do with our minds *matters*. What we think matters. Very often, it determines—or at least plays an important role in determining—what or who we trust. When I believe a person to be wicked, wouldn't it be wrong to trust him? But what happens when we can't believe what we *want* to trust?

James K. A. Smith's excellent book *You Are What You Love* approaches this problem differently but it's the same problem.[3] Smith's most powerful charge is that "we need to become aware of our immersions."[4] We need to recognize we swim in water. Ours is a secular age which trains us to doubt. We learn—from teachers as well as all the little nudges in our surroundings we never notice— to be skeptical, to question everything, to look for proof. We crave knowledge, not faith. Smith recognizes the importance of immersions like these. He proposes re-immersion. He suggests habits are a good way to do it. Our habits shape us. Specifically, they shape

2. Kee, *Way of Transcendence*, 234.

3. Smith, *You Are What You Love*.

4. Smith, *You Are What You Love*, 38.

our love and affections. So one of the central features of Christian spiritual practice should be immersing ourselves in good habits to counteract the formations of our culture.

You'll notice my path for faith without belief deliberately includes habits. Scripture, prayer, Christian community, service, receiving the sacraments: these are all central to immersing ourselves in Christian living. Smith is surely onto something. Our habits shape our loves, desires, and affections. They are formative. So it stands to reason our Christian living may lead us toward Christian belief. Remember, belief is a spectrum and, while we can't choose many of our beliefs, we do choose contexts and habits that form them. The path of faith without belief is faith seeking understanding and, ideally, ends in understanding. It should, that is, help us believe. That's been my experience. Even on a micro level, I notice my doubts subside during weeks when I'm diligently engaged in spiritual practice. I suspect the same will be true for anyone who struggles with severe doubt or nonbelief. It doesn't mean doubt evaporates entirely. But it can tilt us toward belief. Even when it doesn't, the beliefs of the church are our fail-safe option. It's the grace God offers us when all else fails.

You may be disappointed I can't guarantee you belief. I don't have a "ninety days or your money-back guarantee." There's no formula to squash doubt forever. All the good habits and trying to trust may leave you where you started: shrouded in frustratingly static doubt. But one of the promises of Jesus is those who ask, receive. Those who seek, find. What we find may not be what we expected. We may not ever find the kind of convinced belief we read about in books or see in movies. But if we relent and ask Jesus for help in our nonbelief, we may nonetheless find what we seek: God himself relating to us and working in our lives. Thank God, that's enough.

Further Reading

IT TOOK EVERY OUNCE of what little self-control I have not to add a footnote on every sentence to say, "yes, but . . ." or "have you read this book?" Chances are, if you followed the book closely, you noted gaps in my thinking or weaknesses in my arguments. I suppose it's nearly inevitable for a book this size (at least that's what I'm telling myself). To cover that gap, here's an invitation to further reading. It's a combination between a bibliography (these are books which shaped my thinking in this book, even if I didn't quote them) and recommendations (here's a really good book which deals with related themes and you should read it).

The following books fall in one of three categories. First, the academic books. These are the books that *are* stuffed with footnotes. They aren't for everyone, but if you're looking for a more detailed dialogue on some of the conversations we started here, then they could be of use. If I didn't answer a question you have, chances are one of these books does answer it. Second, the popular books. These books *aren't* stuffed with footnotes. In terms of difficulty, they should be in the ballpark of this book (give or take a tick of difficulty). But they are books that helped my own thinking on these issues and could further help yours. Finally, I included a fiction and movies section. Well-told stories can fill out ideas for us in ways nonfiction sometimes cannot. I can give precise definitions and good arguments all day, but a powerful story might be more compelling to some. These aren't just my favorites (though many of these are that, too). These are tales which deal with the themes in this book in one way or another and are worth your time.

Academic Books

Marilyn McCord Adams, *Horrendous Evils and the Goodness of God* | One of the most important books out there on the problem of evil, this is a hard, honest look at the problem which doesn't opt for easy answers.

Matthew Bates, *Salvation by Allegiance Alone* | Maybe more than any other, this book shaped my thinking on how "faith" and "belief" work in the New Testament.

Joshua Cockayne, *Explorations in Analytic Ecclesiology* | Cockayne's book is an excellent resource for thinking deeply about the church across several different themes. One good example is "group agency," which I touched on in this book. Cockayne's exploration of it is much more comprehensive.

Larry Hurtado, *Destroyer of the gods* | Hurtado's exploration of Christianity and books led to his claim that Christianity is a "bookish" religion. But many of the other claims I make about the early church are covered in Hurtado's work.

Derek King, *The Church and the Problem of Divine Hiddenness* | How about a little self-promotion? It feels strange to highlight my own book in a list of otherwise excellent, important books because, well, mine isn't *nearly* as excellent or important. But since I explore similar issues with more detail and rigor, you can go here if you want to know what I think about other issues.

Kevin Kinghorn, *The Decision of Faith* | I was fortunate enough to have Dr. Kinghorn as a professor in seminary. He introduced me to many of the topics I'm writing about today. This book especially explores the extent to which we can choose our beliefs and what it means for faith.

Jonathan Kvanvig, *Faith and Humility* | I'm far from the first person to explore "faith without belief." Kvanvig is a good example of someone who considers the extent to which faith requires certain beliefs.

Joseph Minich, *The Bulwarks of Unbelief* | Riffing off Charles Taylor, Minich further explores the conditions of our culture which invite unbelief.

Paul Moser, *The Elusive God* | Moser invites us to "reorient religious epistemology," or re-evaluate what it means for us to "know" God. Many of the themes in my book show up in Moser somewhere, especially in this book.

Eleonore Stump, *Wandering in Darkness* | An excellent and seemingly comprehensive discussion of the problem of evil. Stump is exceptional at making dense philosophical material readable, interesting, and engaged with Scripture.

Charles Taylor, *A Secular Age* | The massive tome I mention several times. Have fun!

Popular Books

Julie Canlis, *Theology of the Ordinary* | This short little book does an excellent job showing why theology matters for our everyday lives.

Trevor Hart, *Confessing and Believing* | Hart's book is a more expansive version of the Ben Myers *Apostles' Creed* book (listed below). It's an introduction to the basic Christian confession, based on a series of sermons Hart gave (which, as it happens, I was fortunate enough to hear live). The early chapters deal with many of the issues I cover in this book.

C. S. Lewis, *Mere Christianity* | The first two parts, especially, lay out his case for God from morality. But the whole book is a must!

Rebecca McLaughlin, *Confronting Christianity* | Good answers to twelve recurring objections to Christianity. This is straightforward, basic apologetics, which sometimes gets a bad rap these days. But it shouldn't.

Ben Myers, *The Apostles' Creed* | This is as short and introductory as it gets. Myers' book includes short meditations on the different beliefs of the creed and their significance.

James K. A. Smith, *How (Not) to be Secular* | If Charles Taylor's *A Secular Age* is not for the faint of heart, then maybe Smith's short introduction to Taylor's work can be for the semi-faint of heart. Smith gets you the key ideas, so he's a great place to start.

James K. A. Smith, *You Are What You Love* | Smith gets two books here because his work aligns with my own at so many points. This book is especially helpful for considering how our habits and loves are spiritually formative.

Tish Harrison Warren, *The Liturgy of the Ordinary* | Warren's accessible book, like Smith's, considers the "liturgies" of our lives and how to structure our mundane, ordinary lives around God.

Fiction & Movies

Antoine de Saint Exupéry famously said, "If you want to build a ship, don't drum up people to collect wood and don't assign them tasks and work, but rather teach them to long for the endless immensity of the sea." The theology version of this, I guess, is if you want people to have faith in Jesus, don't give them a bunch of arguments, but rather teach them to long for Jesus through the stories we tell. I *do* think the arguments are important. I've personally felt their impact. But, for some, stories are far more compelling and effective. They shape our thinking and imaginations in a way no nonfiction can. Here are some fiction books and movies that have shaped my thinking and imagination as it relates to many of the themes from this book. I'll resist the temptation to give a plug for each one because I'd end up writing another book.

Fiction Books

Brideshead Revisited (Evelyn Waugh)
Diary of a Country Priest (George Bernanos)
Madame Bovary (Gustave Flaubert)
Pride & Prejudice (Jane Austen)
Silence (Shusaku Endo)
The Brothers Karamazov (Fyodor Dostovesky)
Till We Have Faces (C. S. Lewis)

Movies

A Hidden Life (2019)
Babette's Feast (1987)
Calvary (2014)
Rope (1948)
The Banshees of Inisherin (2022)
The Seventh Seal (1957)

Bibliography

Aquinas, Thomas. *Summa Theologiae.* Translated by Laurence Shapcote. Latin/English Edition of the Works of Thomas Aquinas. Green Bay, WI: Aquinas Institute, 2012.

Augustine. *Sermons on the New Testament.* Edited by Philip Schaff. Translated by R. G. MacMullen. Nicene and Post-Nicene Fathers. Buffalo, NY: Christian Literature Publishing Co., 1888. https://www.newadvent.org/fathers/160330.htm.

Bergman, Ingmar, dir. *The Seventh Seal.* 1957. Irvington, NY: Criterion Collection, 2009.

Chesterton, G. K. *Orthodoxy.* San Francisco: Ignatius, 1995.

Cockayne, Joshua. *Explorations in Analytic Ecclesiology: That They May Be One.* Oxford: Oxford University Press, 2023.

Cosmos. PBS, Carl Sagan Productions, British Broadcasting Corporation (BBC), 1980.

Ehrman, Bart D. *The New Testament: A Historical Introduction to the Early Christian Writings.* Oxford: Oxford University Press, 2019.

Flaubert, Gustave. *Madame Bovary.* Translated by Joan Charles. New York: Holt, Rinehart & Winston, 1949.

Hurtado, Larry W. *Destroyer of the gods: Early Christian Distinctiveness in the Roman World.* Waco, TX: Baylor University Press, 2017.

Jacob, Haley Goranson. *Conformed to the Image of His Son: Reconsidering Paul's Theology of Glory in Romans.* Downers Grove, IL: InterVarsity, 2018.

Jackson, Peter, dir. *The Lord of the Rings: The Two Towers.* New Line Cinema, 2002.

James, William. *William James: Writings 1878–1899.* Edited by Gerald E. Myers. New York: Library of America, 1992.

Kee, Alistair. *The Way of Transcendence: Christian Faith Without Belief in God.* Harmondsworth, UK: Penguin, 1971.

Krauss, Lawrence M. *A Universe from Nothing: Why There Is Something Rather than Nothing.* New York: Simon & Schuster, 2013.

Lewis, C. S. *God in the Dock*. Grand Rapids: Eerdmans, 2014.

———. *Letters to Malcolm: Chiefly on Prayer*. Princeton: Mariner, 2002.

———. *Mere Christianity*. San Francisco: HarperSanFrancisco, 2001.

———. *The Silver Chair*. New York, NY: HarperCollins, 2002.

Marshall, Penny, dir. *A League of Their Own*. Columbia Pictures, 1992.

Middleton, J. Richard. *The Liberating Image: The Imago Dei in Genesis 1*. Grand Rapids: Brazos, 2005.

Minich, Joseph. *Bulwarks of Unbelief: Atheism and Divine Absence in a Secular Age*. Bellingham, WA: Lexham Academic, 2023.

Mounce, Robert. *Romans: An Exegetical and Theological Exposition of Holy Scripture*. Nashville: Holman Reference, 1995.

Myers, Ben. *The Apostles' Creed: A Guide to the Ancient Catechism*. Bellingham, WA: Lexham, 2018.

Nagasawa, Yujin. "Silence, Evil, and Shusaku Endo." In *Hidden Divinity and Religious Belief: New Perspectives*, edited by Eleonore Stump and Adam Green, 246–59. Cambridge: Cambridge University Press, 2016.

Sanders, E. P. *The Historical Figure of Jesus*. Reprint ed. New York: Penguin, 1996.

Smith, James K. A. *How (Not) to Be Secular: Reading Charles Taylor*. Grand Rapids: Eerdmans, 2014.

———. *You Are What You Love: The Spiritual Power of Habit*. Grand Rapids: Brazos, 2016.

Spielberg, Steven, dir. *The Terminal*. Dreamworks Pictures, 2004.

Steinbeck, John. *East of Eden*. New York: Penguin, 2002.

Taylor, Charles. *A Secular Age*. Cambridge: Harvard University Press, 2007.

Teresa, Mother. *Mother Teresa: Come Be My Light: The Private Writings of the Saint of Calcutta*. Edited by Brian Kolodiejchuk. New York: Image, 2009.

Vanauken, Sheldon. *A Severe Mercy*. San Francisco: HarperOne, 2009.